Half title page

Detail of late 15th century Altar Frontal with the Tree of Jesse, made in the Cologne region of Germany. The Whitworth Art Gallery, Manchester.

Front Cover ,

Clockwise: St George and the Dragon, *page from an early 16th century French Book of Hours – Blackburn Museum and Art Gallery, Blackburn (Hart Collection); Detail of painted outer coffin of Ta-aaoth, an ancient Egyptian woman, c.1087–664 BC – The Manchester Museum, Manchester;* Arthur Devis, *Portrait of Sir Robert Rich, c.1756–58 – Lancaster City Museum, Lancaster; Detail of reconstructed section of the priory church floor, c.1325 – Norton Priory Museum, Runcorn; Embroidered vanity box, English, c.1655–60 – Abbot Hall Art Gallery, Kendal; L. S. Lowry,* An Accident, *1926 – Manchester City Art Gallery, Manchester; Chelsea porcelain Fable candlestick, 1760 – Carlisle Museum and Art Gallery, Carlisle; Poster advertising Fleetwood – Lancashire County and Regimental Museum, Preston; Sacred baboon – Kendal Museum of Natural History and Archaeology, Kendal.*

Centre right: Figurehead from a brig trading to the West Indies, c.1820 – Lancaster Maritime Museum, Lancaster.

MUSEUMS & GALLERIES COMMISSION

A MUSEUMS ASSOCIATION GUIDE

Exploring
MUSEUMS
North West England
and the Isle of Man

David Phillips

LONDON: HER MAJESTY'S STATIONERY OFFICE

© Crown Copyright 1989
First published 1989
ISBN 0 11 290473 4

British Library Cataloguing in
Publication Data
A CIP catalogue record for this book
is available from the British Library

HMSO BOOKS

HMSO publications are available from:

HMSO Publications Centre
(Mail and telephone orders only)
PO Box 276, London, SW8 5DT
Telephone orders 01–873 9090
General enquiries 01–873 0011
(queuing system in operation for both numbers)

HMSO Bookshops
49 High Holborn, London, WC1V 6HB 01–873 0011 (Counter service only)
258 Broad Street, Birmingham, B1 2HE 021–643 3740
Southey House, 33 Wine Street, Bristol, BS1 2BQ (0272) 264306
9–21 Princess Street, Manchester, M60 8AS 061–834 7201
80 Chichester Street, Belfast, BT1 4JY (0232) 238451
71 Lothian Road, Edinburgh, EH3 9AZ 031–228 4181

HMSO's Accredited Agents
(see Yellow Pages)

and through good booksellers

CONTENTS

OTHER VOLUMES IN THE SERIES

London
Simon Olding (former London
Museums Officer, AMSSEE)
ISBN 0 11 290465 3

South West England
Arnold Wilson (former Director of
Bristol City Art Gallery)
ISBN 0 11 290469 6

North East England
David Fleming (Principal Keeper
of Museums, Hull City Museums
and Art Galleries)
ISBN 0 11 290470 X

The Home Counties
Geoff Marsh, Nell Hoare and
Karen Hull (Museums
Development Officers, AMSSEE)
ISBN 0 11 290471 8

The Midlands
Tim Schadla-Hall (Deputy
Director, Leicestershire
Museums, Art Galleries and
Records Service)
ISBN 0 11 290466 1

East Anglia
Alf Hatton (Lecturer in Museum
Studies at the University of
London)
ISBN 0 11 290472 6

**Southern England
and the Channel Islands**
Kenneth James Barton (former
Director of Hampshire County
Museums Service)
ISBN 0 11 290468 8

Scotland
Colin Thompson (former Director
of National Galleries of Scotland
and former Chairman of the
Scottish Museums Council)
ISBN 0 11 290474 2

Ireland
Seán Popplewell (Executive
Director, Irish Museums Trust)
ISBN 0 11 290475 0

Wales
Geraint Jenkins (Curator, Welsh
Folk Museum)
ISBN 0 11 290467 X

BUCKINGHAM PALACE

As Patron of Museums Year 1989, I hope that through this series of Regional Guides "Exploring Museums", you will derive great enjoyment from the fascinating world of museums and galleries; there are some two thousand of them offering an immense variety and range of experiences so there is something for everyone. It is so exciting to feel the sense of exploring new areas in the world of museums and galleries. Make the most of what is on offer in 1989.

Sarah.

January 1989

EDITOR'S NOTE

This volume is one of a series of eleven regional guides to museums in the British Isles. The term 'museum' is often applied to a wide variety of collections and buildings: most of the places selected for description in the *Exploring Museums* guides, however, comply as far as possible with the Museums Association's definition of a museum as 'an institution that collects, documents, preserves, exhibits and interprets material evidence and associated information for the public benefit'.

Given the sheer quantity of museums in the British Isles, the guides describe only a selection, concentrating on those places that authors considered most worthy of a visit, either because of the quality of their collections and displays, or because of the interesting or unusual nature of what they have on view. Museums in each area not described in full are listed at the back of the guides, with brief details of their collections; please note that some of these are only open by appointment. The lists include new museums that are scheduled to open in the near future.

The principal aim of this series is to describe, through words and pictures, the types of things that visitors can expect to see and do at various museums. Authors have tried to put themselves in the shoes of a general museum visitor, and present a personal rather than an official view in their descriptions. It should be noted that specific items they describe may not be on show when you visit: most museums now change their displays fairly often, and if you want to see something in particular you should check beforehand with the museum concerned. Most of the illustrations have been selected by the authors, and highlight lesser-known objects and museum activities, as well as exhibits for which particular museums are renowned. Basic information about access and facilities has been kept to a minimum, as opening times or bus routes, for example, are frequently subject to change; please check with museums before visiting for precise details of opening times, holiday closures, admission prices, and how to get there, and for information on special events and activities.

Krystyna Matyjaszkiewicz
Series Editor

The views expressed in this guide are those of the author and not necessarily those of the Museums Association.

FOREWORD

President of the Museums Association
Patrick Boylan
and the Chairman of the Museums & Galleries Commission
Brian Morris

This series is being published in Museums Year 1989, which marks the centenary of the Museums Association. When the Association's first conference was held in York in 1889, there were already several hundred museums in Britain. Now there are some 2,300, and new ones are opening every month. They vary enormously in size and scope, from the large all-purpose museum to the small collection in a converted house. Many of the smaller museums are less well known than they should be, and it is these particularly that the books in this series seek to highlight.

Museums Year 1989, sponsored by The Times newspaper, represents the most significant promotion of the country's museums and galleries ever staged. Through their sponsorship Museums Year will bring fresh vitality to a particularly important part of our British heritage.

Never before have museums in general been as popular as they are today. In 1989 alone they are expected to receive between them something like 100 million visits (which is more than any sport or other leisure activity). They are especially attractive to young people, to the curious of all ages and to the lovers of beautiful, unusual and exciting things. There are indeed museums for every taste and interest, for every day and in every area. We are sure that these books will help many more people to discover the museums of Britain, to learn from them and to enjoy them.

INTRODUCTION

The story of the north west of England is one of extremes, intensive industry contrasting with spectacular landscape, immense wealth with extreme poverty. It offers wonderful opportunities for museums, which have been developed all over the area in a wealth of imaginative ways during the last century. Developments have never been more rapid or imaginative than they are now. Indeed displays, and in some cases whole museums, are changing so quickly that some of the ones described here have been transformed even as we go to press. Readers who set out to use the main entries in this book strictly as a guide may therefore be disappointed. It shouldn't matter, though; for when visiting any museum we should beware of allowing ourselves to be led, whether by a guidebook, by acres of fearfully educational labelling, or by high-tech information aids.

The older presentations you find in most museums may be more an accident of history than the fruits of planning. Take the traditional municipal museums, all the stuffed animals in one bit, the art somewhere else; they were certainly meant to be planned, and were set up primarily with the popular audience in mind. One might have expected them to take a heavily educational approach. The local councils that put up the cash for such museums had hard-headed, if somewhat optimistic aims: they hoped that lots of stuffed birds and *objets d'art* of an edifying kind would draw the working classes from the public houses, and improve the quality and, therefore, competitiveness of manufactures with a decorative content, such as textiles and ceramics.

Any chance of getting this improbable message across vanished, because in presenting their new collections most curators unfortunately followed an earlier and very unsuitable pattern. A number of the first municipal museums incorporated the collections of local scientific societies, and the new curators took as models of good practice, for works of art as well as for scientific specimens, the conventions of acquisition and display appropriate to the scholarly study of science and natural history. Much scientific discovery has depended on systematically collecting all the varieties of things of a particular kind, and arranging them in arrays so as to try to demonstrate the relationships within and between specimens: all the molluscs you can get hold of are set out in one place, all lepidoptera in another, and so on. Applied to public collections of the arts, the procedure was a catastrophe, but one we still live with: paintings grouped separately by school; teapots all in a show case somewhere; snuff-boxes stored in drawers; every specimen with a neat, or not so neat, identifying label and number.

Even when they are planned, however excellently, museum displays should never be taken at face value. For the way an object is displayed is bound to affect the meanings that are attached to it. This is clearly true where a long label spells out why a curator thinks an item is important; but even displaying objects with no obvious explanations can affect what they seem to signify. An especially poignant example are the treasures from Asia or Africa that we occasionally come across in some of the older regimental history displays. Here, they are mere trophies, along with Napoleon's buttons and German machine-guns. They may tell us something about the Imperial past and the military mind, but they tell us nothing about the cultures from which they came. Almost identical items will convey a quite different impression if seen in a modern ethnographic display, with other artefacts from the same cultures. Even then, if the people who made and used them were to come to the museum, they would probably find the inclusion in museum displays of what are often ritual objects totally meaningless, and perhaps offensive. However we display an object, we change what it means, and often in the process we say more about ourselves than we do about the object.

The same goes for other kinds of display, which may impose messages by omission or commission. There are many curators, especially of paintings and the decorative arts, who resist disturbing their arrays of specimens with more than the odd typed label, full of rather arcane art-historical lore; information can intrude, and they feel that objects should be left to speak for themselves. Others feel that some museum exhibits, especially works of art or objects from everyday life and work, should not be allowed to speak for themselves because they express particular social or political views that are now unacceptable; they feel that to display them without comment is to endorse these unacceptable attitudes. Others, again, argue that this is absurd, since objects left to speak for themselves are simply inaudible to most of us. But displays that successfully combine exhibits with explanations are even more prone to becoming outdated. Take the educational displays that energetic curators of science and natural history devised early this century, with lots of labels and diorama backgrounds; many present the world of nature as a limitless resource awaiting only our technological exploitation. Nothing could be further from the message of more recent displays (such as the one in **Kendal Museum**), which try to explain it as a delicate linked system that we disturb at our peril.

You might think you could hardly go wrong by just leaving a few looms and a steam engine in a closed-down mill. But even this can be misread. There is great debate about whether the recent 'heritage' museums and sites tend to present a rosy view of the past. A good, entirely unintended example of this is at **Styal Mill**, in the kitchen of the house in which the eighty orphaned or abandoned apprentices lived. The museum staff there are at pains to emphasise how grindingly hard and tedious life must have been, both for the workers in the kitchen, and for the children they fed. They know how hard it is, because they regularly prepare food in the primitive conditions. Yet in spite of all their efforts, we visitors love it: the stone-flagged floor and scrubbed wood tables, the fire in the open range, the herbs hanging from the ceiling, the simple earthenware vessels – it all looks like the most desirable kitchen in a colour supplement fantasy cottage. We forget the orphans, the cold water, the skin raw with preparing vegetables, and we dream of the good life. If this is the effect where staff specifically try to avoid stressing the charm of the site, the intensity of the rosy tint in displays where it is played up can be understood. This might not matter, some commentators feel, but for the risk that the rosy glow may spread to include the whole apprenticeship system, and all kinds of attitudes that are now widely seen as questionable.

By now you, the potential visitor may be thoroughly alarmed. Even those wonderfully empty traditional galleries, undisturbed except for the secret meetings of lovers and spies, may be indoctrinating you with socially unacceptable attitudes. The bright face of more recent displays, and the visitor amenities of heritage attractions, may be lulling you into unquestioning political acquiescence. But perhaps these messages do not really get through to us visitors, any more than did the improvement that the Victorians hoped all those stuffed birds would inspire in their audience.

In any case, the answer is that just as you should never trust anything simply because it is in print, you should never take too seriously the lessons presented by museums. They may be the main attraction if you have gone to a museum as you might go to a library, needing to get the orthodox line on something, perhaps to help with an educational course project. Even then, as in any lesson, avoid its errors and bring it alive by asking your own questions, and taking any answers supplied with a pinch of salt. Museums really come into their own when you cease to let yourself be led around them, being presented with objects and information, and start making your own discoveries. A visit becomes alive, becomes an experience one could have nowhere else, when you suddenly find your attention totally occupied by some unexpected object, or a whole display of whatever style, because it seems to you strange, or moving, or beautiful. The main entries here are meant to offer an impression of one set of discoveries, bristling, I hope, with enough bias and prejudice to provoke you into going and seeing for yourself.

David Phillips

ACKNOWLEDGEMENTS

Author's acknowledgements

In preparing this book, I found two existing guides particularly helpful: British Leisure Publications' *Museums and Galleries in Great Britain and Ireland*, and Kenneth Hudson and Ann Nicholls' *Cambridge Guide to the Museums of Britain and Ireland*. For our book, I am grateful to the many museum people who have gone to a great deal of trouble to supply pictures, and to purge the text of as many as possible of my errors. Ian Wolfenden kindly read much of the manuscript, and suggested a number of important improvements. Krystyna Matyjaszkiewicz has been a very supportive and perceptive editor.

Photographic acknowledgements

The Museums Association is grateful to all the museums, archives and photographers who generously provided material for illustration herein. Photographs were supplied by, and are reproduced courtesy of, the respective museums and their governing bodies or Trustees, except for those noted below.

p. 12 (Burnley), photograph of kitchen range © copyright *Lancashire Life* 1981; pp. 18–20 and colour plate 13 (Ellesmere Port), photographs lent by and reproduced courtesy of The Boat Museum Archive Collection; pp. 20–22 and colour plate 9 (Grasmere), photographs © copyright and reproduced courtesy of The Wordsworth Trust; pp. 28–30 (Kendal Museum, and Museum of Lakeland Life and Industry), photographs of Woodland scene, Kendal window, Chemist's shop and Newspaper boy © copyright *Westmorland Gazette*; p. 48 (Walker Art Gallery), David Hockney's *Peter getting out of Nick's Pool*, 1967 © copyright David Hockney 1967; pp. 80–81 (Runcorn), photographs © copyright and reproduced courtesy of Norton Priory Museum Trust; p. 100 (Manx Museum), Viking ship model a gift of the Friends of Manx Museum, illustrates a type of ship in which Vikings came to the Isle of Man, and is a scale model of the Gokstad ship, made in Oslo under the supervision of the man who set up the original vessel in the Viking Ship Museum.

Key to Symbols Used

F Free admission

£ Admission charge

V Voluntary donation requested

▣ Restaurant/cafeteria on premises

P Car Park on premises

♿ Good access and facilities for disabled

♿ Difficult/limited access and facilities for disabled and infirm

> **W** Unstepped access via main or side door, wheelchair spaces, and adapted toilet
>
> **T** Adapted toilet
>
> **X** Flat or one-step access
>
> **A** Access with 2–5 steps, or split level exhibition space
>
> **S** Many unavoidable steps and/ or other obstacles for wheelchair users and the infirm
>
> **G** Provision made for guide dogs
>
> (based on disabled access code devised by ARTSLINE (01 388 2227), the free telephone information service on the arts in Greater London for people with disabilities)

⚤ Group visits

⚤ School group visits

◎ Workshops/holiday events/ guided tours/talks – 'phone for details

Museums shown in **bold** type in the text are described in full elsewhere in the volume; those shown in *italic* type are briefly described in the list of museums and collections at the back.

ACCRINGTON

Haworth Art Gallery

*Haworth Park, Manchester Road,
Accrington, Lancashire
BB5 2JS   (0254) 33782*
Closed every morning and all day
Fridays. **F P**
&ST: wheelchair access to ground
floor only, but staff will assist any
disabled person to see the Tiffany
Collection.
& please phone in advance;
bookings can also be accepted
sometimes for morning and
evening visits by school parties,
clubs and organisations.

Accrington might not spring to mind as
the obvious place in England to see
some of the most extravagantly opulent
glassware ever made, a collection of
130 pieces from the workshops of
Louis Comfort Tiffany. But the building that houses the collection is, quite
by coincidence, not inappropriate at all.
The house was built in 1909 for William and Anne Haworth, cotton industrialists, by Walter Brierley, an
architect who specialised in less compact accommodation for the self-made

An opalescent Tiffany lamp

John Frederick Herring Sr, My Ladye's Palfrey, *1849*

magnate. Brierley clearly had an eye
for the one thing missing in the lives of
these men-who-had-everything: family
roots. Nothing more suggestive of a
well-rooted family tree could be devised than the 'Olde Englande' Elizabethan appearance of Hollins Hill, as
this house was called; only the uncom-
promisingly straight edges and smooth
surfaces of the best workmanship
Edwardian money could buy add a
modern touch to his feast of carving,
crenellation and stags' heads. William
and Anne Haworth filled the house
with good pictures, which remain, and
have been further added to by gift from
local families, now that the house is
used as a gallery for the locality,
according to the Haworth's wishes.
Most are solidly Victorian, by such
figures as Herring, Shayer and Birkett-
Foster, but there is a fine French 18th
century storm scene, by Claude Joseph
Vernet.
   A Tiffany collection suits such a
house because Tiffany addressed in
America much the same market as
Brierley in northern England. Roots
were not so important there, but having
the best that money could buy certainly

was. Tiffany was the best, and there
was a lot of money about. Born into the
jewellery business of 'Breakfast at Tiffany's' fame, Louis Comfort Tiffany
(1812–1902) became an interior de-
corator, after coming to terms with not
being the greatest painter. He devised
interiors for the most stylish people in a
stylish age, and commissions included
Mark Twain's house, the Vanderbilt
Mansion and the White House. Tiffany's clients were not after restraint,
which suited his own taste fine. He
became interested in glass technology
while searching for ever more glowing
stained-glass effects in his interiors,
and as his interest grew he was able to
pay for unprofitable experimentation
through his interior decorating business. By the early 1890s he had
absorbed various influences from the
arts of North Africa and the Orient,
while inspiration for glass design had
come from the Arts and Crafts movement in England, which rejected in-
dustrialised ornamental processes, and
from novel Art Nouveau methods in
European glassmaking.
   Accrington got in on the act around
1890, when a 17-year-old calico block

maker, Joseph Briggs, crossed the Atlantic and got a job in Tiffany's glassmaking business. He became an art director at the time of its heyday, around the turn of the century, and kept on part of the business when tastes changed and Tiffanyware became unfashionable during the 1920s and '30s, and when the ageing Tiffany himself had withdrawn, disgusted with trends in contemporary design. There was so little demand for the glassware by this time that quantities of it were simply destroyed, but Accrington gladly accepted half of Briggs's own collection, and this was added to by pieces from relatives, to whom he had made gifts.

Glass chemistry in general was very much in the melting pot during the years when Tiffany was developing his particular effects. Makers of optical glass for lenses were finding that the way light behaved in glass could be controlled precisely through the addition to the basic glass mixture of exotic substances. The chemistry behind the firework effects of Tiffanyware was just as hard-headed, even if the results look more like alchemy. Tiffany liked the alchemy to show, and most of the finishes that he especially admired

were the end product of a whole series of chemical reactions that happened not in the space enclosed by a test-tube, but in the body of the glass itself, or on its surface.

The results often imitate the appearance of glassware from the ancient Mediterranean. Irridescence occurs naturally on the surface of some ancient glass with time, and Tiffany's craftsmen developed a repertoire of lustrous finishes to imitate this natural phenomenon: salts of rare metals dissolved in the glass mixture were conjured to the surface of wares, sprayed with metal chloride and re-heated. Similar wizardry produced the other imitations of ancient glass, such as Cypriote, Lava and Agate. Almost all the effects emerged literally in the heat of the moment, leaving no scope for reworking or laborious finishing work, which might give tell-tale deadness to the surface.

Accrington's collection is the largest in Europe, and one of the finest in the world; it includes examples of many of the most celebrated product types. Briggs was particularly associated at first with the mosaic-glass-panel side of the business, and one such panel, 'Sulphur Crested Cockatoos', is in the

A fine aquamarine Tiffany vase

collection. It resembles some of the effects introduced in painting by followers of the Impressionists: the little slabs of irridescent glass, of which the mosaic is composed, change colour as you move, building up an image composed of a multitude of patches of contrasting colour. There is one of the famous vases with blue peacock-feather decoration combed into it, and one of the gold 'Jack-in-the-Pulpit' vases, with a lily-like leaf unfolding at the top of a tall, slim stem. In recent years the museum has managed to acquire one of the famous lamps, with shades of leaded coloured glass; every home should have one, and during the great age of Tiffany, just about everyone did. Examples of modern glass are also being acquired to extend the range of the museum's collections.

The Tiffany collection makes a trip to Accrington a must for the specialist, but the gallery is an attractive place to visit for anyone. It is set in its own park just outside the centre of town, and is a more than usually active centre of local artistic life, with many rooms given over to a lively exhibition programme showing in particular work by local artists and crafts people.

Three Tiffany 'lava glass' vases

ASHTON-UNDER-LYNE

Portland Basin Industrial Heritage Centre

1 Portland Place, Portland Street South, Ashton-under-Lyne, Tameside, Lancashire OL6 7SY
(061) 308 3374
Closed Mondays. 🅵 🅿 ♿
🚻 & 🚻 contact museum for details.

Portland Basin is an atmospherically sited new museum of the social and economic history of Tameside. The displays are housed in the former warehouse of the Ashton Canal Company, rebuilt after a fire of 1972 which destroyed all but the ground floor, and sited strategically at a junction of three canals. The museum's collections are small but growing. Items already acquired are cleverly used to illustrate and enliven a quantity of imaginatively presented panels of information and photographs. These present the early history of settlement here, which began relatively late since the area is part foothills, part plain, and was marginal land until about the 13th century. In this terrain wool became the first staple of wealth. But wool gave way to cotton in the later 18th century when the cotton industry developed rapidly in Lancashire because of the advantages that the area offered for cotton manu-

View of the Forge

Bowton's Yard, Stalybridge, 1933

facture: textile expertise in a workforce that was not organised into guilds and associations; a wet climate, important for spinning cotton thread; and coal available locally for fuel. Lancashire soon came to dominate the world's cotton trade; it was said that the County produced England's needs before breakfast, the rest of the world's for the remainder of the day. But the cotton industry was not a particularly forward looking one, and the area has suffered hard with the decline of the industry since the 1930s.

The museum's panels present many aspects of the story in knowledgeable detail, from doing the washing to going to the pub, political protest to local government, making clogs to mining coal. There is on display a case of beautiful woodworking tools, almost entirely of turned and carved wood; a fine washing machine and mangle; and fittings from a traditional fish and chip shop. There are also examples of the diesel engines that became a local speciality once the blacksmiths of the earlier economy developed their metalworking expertise for the new mechanical industry.

The display is especially good on the radical movement called Chartism. It still comes as a shock to realise that most people of any position in society as late as 1840 regarded as a dangerous firebrand anyone in favour of voting rights for all adult males (let alone for women), and of voting by ballot, of a reasonable distribution of electoral districts, and of the right of members of parliament to be paid, and not to have to be property holders. The only point of the charter, after which the movement is named, that we would not now take for granted was a proposal that elections be annual.

More down to earth, there is a good section on clogs, essential foot protection for dangerous work in a damp climate. They were not all wooden, like Dutch clogs, but had leather uppers and metal base-plates on soles of carved alder-wood. They were not just for work, but became part of recreational culture for a society that had to rely on invention rather than purchasing power for entertainment. Clogs were grand for dancing, on slate to bring out the sound. They were good for 'purring' too – kicking matches, decided by the surrender of one or other contestant, a favourite with the miners.

These displays are all on the ground floor. A mezzanine floor, under arrangement at the time of writing, will present more displays, especially of hatting, and temporary exhibitions, as well as providing space for educational work.

The Basin itself is a triangular pool, surrounded by a mixture of greenery and sternly impressive industrial buildings. Three canals lead from it, west into Manchester, east to Huddersfield, and south to the quarries of the Peak district and on to the Midlands. The west and southern routes were not easily built: the tunnels of the Huddersfield canal, expected to take five years to excavate, took sixteen and a half; the Peak Forest canal relied on a sequence of locks to cope with the steep climb to the Peaks. Nevertheless, these canals enjoyed prosperity for

Canal boat, with the Whittle family

twenty years or so, until the development of the railways defeated them. The management of all three canals was in the hands of their rivals, the railway companies, by the end of the 1840s, and the new managements saw to it that they never prospered again. A boatman, quoted in the displays, recalls that the lock-keepers installed by the railway companies were notoriously unhelpful, and that dredging was neglected, so as to reduce the carrying capacity of the canals.

The restored site is an atmospheric spot to visit. There is a grand water-wheel now in working order, once used to power the hoists for the warehouse. Walks along the tow-paths are linked by bridges, one of them, opposite the warehouse – a low arc over the mouth of the Peak Forest Canal – an especially graceful example. A wander up the tow-path to the south offers a special spectacle: the canal at this point is carried by an aqueduct over the river Tame, thirty-odd feet below, and the effect of water flowing by on different levels is rather odd.

BIRKENHEAD

Williamson Art Gallery

Slatey Road, Birkenhead, Wirral L43 4UE   (051) 652 4177
Open daily, and till 9pm on Thursdays. 🄵 🄿   ♿
♿ & ♿ phone to give notice and discuss special requirements, including refreshments.

The Williamson Art Gallery has two very different special collections: one is of ceramics, offering a chance to get to know local Della Robbia and Liverpool Pottery, and the other is of ship models. The gallery also has a rather unusual collection of pictures, and interesting local history displays. Two galleries are devoted to temporary exhibitions, of which there are about thirty a year, some of local interest and others more general. In addition, the gallery is currently the temporary home of the Baxter collection of motoring history, whilst a permanent site for it is established. The collection includes a representative array of motorbikes, and some vintage cars, such as an Austin 7 Opal, displayed in a good reconstruc-

Vanessa Bell, Interior with Housemaid, *1939*

tion of a garage workshop. Apart from this display, the permanent collections are shown in a rather traditional manner, which enables visitors with an enthusiasm for the gallery's specialities to make exciting discoveries for themselves.

The pictures in the collection fall into three groups. First are the oil paintings, by English and continental artists of the Victorian period. Charles Napier Hemy's 'Silent Adieu' is typically moody. A girl in a cottage garden looks sadly over her shoulder as her lover vanishes into the dusk; but this is no ordinary cottage garden, for the gate opens directly onto what seems to be deep-water sea, and the vanishing lover is on the schooner that we see close by. Has he boarded via the garden gate? The effect is a bit surrealistic, and irresistably atmospheric. Another oddity is an 'Interior with a Self Portrait of the Artist' by Robert George Kelly. Who, you ask? He is now just a name on lists of occasional exhibitors in the 19th century, but was no struggling pauper, at any rate not to begin with. The interior is a huge salon, hung with drapes, with reminders all around of the great art that the extremely young painter aspires to emulate. There is a statue of Hercules, a vast painting of the humiliated St. Peter failing to walk on the water, and a prominent copy of the lectures of Sir Joshua Reynolds, just about the ultimate authority on academic standards in painting. Kelly reads thoughtfully, a composition in which we can make out the unmistakeable person of Jesus sketched on his easel. Similar dramas and melodramas are played out in many of the paintings here, and there is a rarity in England, a painting of the great Leo Tolstoy in his garden, by a Russian painter of his time, J.A. Vladimiroff.

In a room to themselves are a second group of paintings, also of the Victorian era, but by painters of the Liverpool School. Quite a large number of artists associated with the area specialised in an extremely detailed manner of painting, following the prescription of the great critic of the time, John Ruskin. John Brett is the most distinguished of

Model of the twin-screw train ferry, 'Leonard', built at Cammell Lairds

Model of the ferry, 'Hinterton'

them represented here, with marvellously painted sand-dunes in his 'Two rivals at Anglesea'. There is a rare work by John J. Lee, a painter of pictures whose titles sound painfully sentimental: 'Sweethearts and Wives' in the **Walker Art Gallery**, Liverpool, is the best known, and here is 'Grandfather's Comfort'. The paintings themselves, though, are understated. They are dominated by faces, impassive but intensely observed and characterised, in a way that makes them far more expressive of real drama and emotion than most pictures of the period.

The same cannot be said for the works of George Lance. He specialised in rather clumsily painted still-lives exuding theatrical opulence. No banal peeling of vegetables is allowed to low-

er the tone of 'Preparation for a Banquet'. The maid is about to pluck a swan, no less, with the look of one who has done this sort of thing often enough to spare a glance for her kitchen-boy companion, whilst he teases a cat with a peacock's tail feather that just happens to be lying about. Hard though it might seem to go further over the top than George Lance, the carved oak furniture of the 1880s in the room devoted to these painters achieves it, in a festival of grotesque black bulges, knobbles and twists.

The third group of pictures are the English 19th century watercolours. The gallery has a large collection of rather showy examples, with a few excellent items. There are, for instance, good examples by three artists

A selection of Della Robbia pottery

BLACKBURN

Blackburn Museum and Art Gallery

*Museum Street, Blackburn,
Lancashire BB1 7AJ
(0254) 667130*
Closed Sundays and Mondays. ▣
& S: wheelchair access very limited.
🚻 & 🍴 phone to give notice of large parties, and for details of services.

Blackburn's Museum and Art Gallery is a monument to late 19th century civic confidence in progress through improvement of the populace. It was built as the free library and museum, in the gothic manner appropriate for a building enshrining the civilised virtues, but with relief sculptural panels at first-floor level outside, presenting elevating scenes of industry and science. The entrance doorway is more artistic, with fine art-nouveau period scrolled wrought ironwork, and mosaics.

Inside, turning to the left, we enter a passageway, or time-tunnel, offering glimpses through windows into tableaux from the past. Amongst them are a clog-maker's shop; a parlour from around 1900; and an especially good bathroom, with dark-wood panelled bath and lavatory, and a fine flowered sink on a cast-iron stand. The tin of carbolic tooth-powder in the latter does not look good to wake up to, but is characteristic of the attention to detail in these reconstructions. Further down the passage is some natural history and enthnographic material, including a singularly fearsome straw ceremonial figure, identified as West-African. Nearby is an imaginative case of mystery objects – things like candle-snuffers, whose strange forms are puzzling for anyone born too recently to guess what they might have been used for, in a world without electricity. Emerging again into the main downstairs hall we find more local history

who liked to use the medium to record their delight in unusual shapes. Samuel Palmer (best known generally because Tom Keating forged his work in particular) is represented by a farm-yard scene full of strange details observed with the utmost precision; the shape of the tree, growing out of the thatched shed, and the plough in the right foreground are especially notable. In John Sell Cotman's study of a ruined priory, every wall leans, and odd patterns of stonework and timber framing reveal adaptations to the masonry. There is a rapid sketch by John Ruskin, too, of one of the Alpine rock formations that fascinated him, this one of limestone. Each of these artists was so acute an observer that from their work one could reconstruct in fine detail the three-dimensional shapes of what they show; yet each has a powerfully individual and rapid style.

The ceramic collections offer a striking contrast. The Liverpool porcelain of 1775 to 1806 is delicately thin, with decoration painted or transfer-printed onto a cold white background. The Della Robbia wares made in Birkenhead at the end of the last century are exuberant, and mostly ornamental, with many large dishes and vases, their decoration in general typically Art Nouveau. They are in heavy earthenware, with strong patterns, earthy colours for the most part, and high glazes. Some of the decoration is painted, some incised. A lizard is modelled in relief on one jug, whose

handle is in the form of a monster. Flowing hair on figures and meandering stems on other pieces are typical for the period.

Shipbuilding and Birkenhead have been synonymous for a long time. Some of the ship models in the central room of the museum are of the ferries that linked the towns of the Wirral shore with Liverpool, others are of ships built in the great Cammel Laird shipyards. There is a row of what are called 'plating half models', sectioned hulls of ships under construction, with a carefully-drawn mosaic of plates that provided the measurements for the metal cladding plates of the real thing. Numerous ships, some famous, like the 'Mauretania', are represented by complete models, and there are some exotica too. The shipyard produced a floating dry-dock in 1912, for the Admiralty, big enough for battleships, and a double-decker ferry that had to also act as an ice-breaker, for getting trains across Canada.

Some of the ferry models are in a room full of bygones of old Birkenhead – maps, pictures, a cast of the footprints of a prehistoric Cheirotherium, and the Town Clerk's wig, which looks as it if it saw some action. Best of all, you can put 5p into a vintage musical pier-end entertainment machine, a Polyphon; in return, a wheel punched with a pattern of holes trips levers to play melancholy Edwardian airs, like the intermezzo 'Xenia' or 'The Old Brigade'.

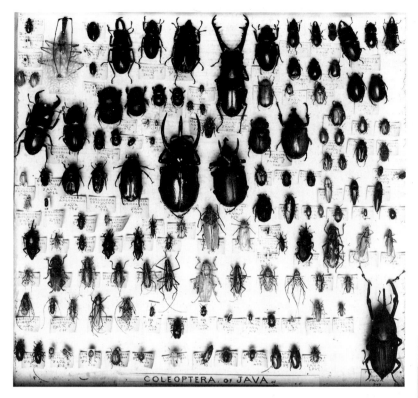

Drawer of beetles

Japanese woodcut by Hiroshige, Sudden Shower at Shono, *c.1833/34 (Lewis Collection)*

displays, and a room for temporary exhibitions at the back of the museum. Beyond the staircase is a gallery full of the uniforms and medals, captured guns and artefacts, accumulated by the East Lancashire Regiment. Amongst many actions, they took part in the punitive raid on Benin, in Nigeria, after an English party establishing unwelcome trading links had been attacked. The punitive expedition took a terrible revenge, and brought away a mass of booty from the rich and sophisticated culture of the region, now displayed as trophies in so many regimental museums. The East Lancs. bagged a magnificent elephant tusk, carved with the figures of warriors.

Upstairs, on the landing, is a long and ancient case containing a splendid, truly vintage display of *Coleoptera*, or beetles, from all over the world. This is a real feast of specimens, packed together but carefully sorted and arranged, each with a tiny, handwritten identifying label. There are minute ones and colossal ones, some unremarkable to a layman's eye, others with giant shiny jaws and curving horns. The colours and textures are wonderful. How stylish it would be to go out looking like black, stripey *Tefflue Megerle*. Especially curious is *Coleorrhina oberthuri*, with irridescent wingcases, which at first glance appear translucent. To the left is another small room, full of stuffed birds.

The three large rooms on the upper floor are devoted to the art gallery. Blackburn is well furnished with ceramics, English watercolours and Victorian oil paintings of the kind generally held to be just the thing to improve the public when museums like this were established. The watercolours include works by Varley, Turner and Callow. Amongst the oils is a picture of romance in the Regency period, painted for the Victorian age by Marcus Stone. Called 'Two's Company, Three's None', it shows a woman withdrawing, perhaps sadly, so as to leave undisturbed in a garden a couple who clearly have some things to sort out between them. On the back (not visible, of course), is a note from the artist saying how glad he is that the borough museum committee is contemplating its purchase, since he considers it his best picture. The effect is lessened now that it is known that he sent precisely the same sentiment to the committee in Nottingham when they acquired their Marcus Stone. Also here is one of the most glittering of the strange mosaic-like paintings of little girls trapping butterflies at the seaside, which Edward Hornel established as a profitable speciality early this century, in a style that he invented after a study of Japanese art. As well as paintings, the collection of works of art of this period includes fine Venetian glassware, especially vases by the firm of Salviati, with exotic horse-head and dragon handles.

Blackburn also has three very special and unusual collections. The first is of Japanese woodcut prints, mostly of the later 18th and early 19th centuries. Prints of this kind only became well known to the West quite late in the last century, because their exquisite qualities of patterning suggested artistic effects that seemed to offer new directions for many artists in England and on the Continent. The best-known Japanese artist of the school is Hokusai, a polymath with a vast output. Blackburn has landscapes and figure subjects by him, and by all the other major artists of the school as well. These prints were made for the popular market in Japan, to the extent of being looked down upon by connoisseurs, and most artists specialised in subject matter reflecting some chosen preoccupations of popular culture. Utamaro presented the daily life of notoriously beautiful women, who in Japan at the time tended to become not actresses but sophisticated courtesans. Sharaku specialised in portraits of actors and actresses, Kuniyoshi and Kunisada in scenes from legend and drama, shown in the latest, vivid chemical dyes.

Most remarkable of all, recently reinstalled in a room of its own with modern fittings, is the collection of coins, illuminated manuscripts and fine printed books, which was the lifetime passion of Robert Edward Hart. Collecting clearly meant a lot more to Hart

Venetian glass bowl by Salviati, 19th century

than did the family rope-making business, which provided the funds. Because illuminated manuscripts fade quickly if much exhibited, and are in any case usually in fragile volumes, it is not often realised what a large and flourishing business their manufacture was, especially in northern Europe around 1500. Hundreds of thousands of little volumes, especially Books of 'Hours', recording the devotions appropriate for different times of day, were decorated with pictures and decorative panels of flowers and creatures (ill. on cover). They added a touch of consumer gratification to the supposedly pious lives of the families of the well-to-do. The standards of draughtsmanship were not always high, and it is fun to try to decide which of the illuminations in such books were by artists who could not paint them fast enough, and which by artists who cared. Hart's collection is also rich in books full of the printed pictures that put a stop to this business, from

Dances of Death in the early 16th century, to William Morris's spectacularly decorated edition of Chaucer in 1896. Hart's coins, finally, are displayed so that we can study the hairstyles of the empresses in ancient Rome, and see the coinage on which nearly twenty centuries of English monarchs stamped their likenesses, as a daily reminder of who was boss. What goods or services you wonder, were exchanged for this penny of the reign of Alfred, the half-noble of Richard II, or the groat of Henry VIII?

The third special collection, and the most recent to be displayed, is that of Greek and Russian Orthodox icons (colour plate 1). The paintings are on show in a mezzanine above the Hart collection, and constitute the largest display of icons in this country. With the illuminated manuscripts below, it is quite interesting to compare the different approaches of Eastern and Western Christian churches to the representation of holy images.

BOLTON

Bolton Museum and Art Gallery

Le Mans Crescent, Bolton BL1 1SE
(0204) 22311 ext. 2191
Closed Wednesdays and Sundays.
🅵 🖻
♿ W: via ramp at entrance, then public lift to all galleries except Natural History, access to which is by arrangement, via another lift.
🚻 & 🚻 phone (ext. 2193) to give notice of visit, and to discuss special requirements and available services.

Nobody could accuse the premises that house Bolton's main museum and art gallery of being cosy. The galleries are on the first floor at one end of a crescent of late 1930s municipal buildings, with the magistrates' court at the other end, the library on the ground floor below the gallery, and the cafeteria in the basement. A steady

Henry Moore, Helmet Head no. 5 (Giraffe), *1966*

stream of visitors, however (especially on Saturdays) climb the grand staircase to see very good natural history collections, artefacts from many non-European cultures, particularly ancient Egypt, and an art collection that includes some very good English watercolours and ceramics, and outstanding contemporary craft pottery. Two large galleries are devoted to temporary exhibitions, often of contemporary art, with intermittent major shows on the subject of individual watercolourists, or aspects of the art of the past.

A brightly lit display of 20th century sculpture has been installed in the main hall. There are several pieces by Henry Moore, and portraits by Jacob Epstein. George Bernard Shaw was fascinated but puzzled by his portrait; he felt that it showed him as a primitive barbarian, and was a projection into his features of Epstein's own wild personality. Other pieces here are by Lynn Chadwick, Eduardo Paolozzi and Elizabeth Frink.

The gallery's watercolours offer an opportunity to trace the way that use of the medium changed as it became established, by the time of Turner, as a medium for exhibition works, not just for studies. Thomas Serres's study of 'Chelsea Waterworks' shows the 18th century use of watercolour. First the whole scene was painted in, complete with shadows, in monochrome grey. Then blue for the sky and earth colours for the sails and timbers were washed as a tint over the top.

Turner began his career playing with delicate effects of this kind, but heightened the contrasts as he moved to subjects that suggested ever greater antiquity, and ever more dramatic spaces. 'Logging on the Upper Rhine' is a good example of this later work. The logging is taking place in a huge ravine, crowned with fortifications on either side, all in a golden haze. By this time Turner had long abandoned the 18th century monochrome underdrawing and tinted colour tradition in which he had been trained. The surface is built up on a blurry mist of strong colour, applied wet, run together, then sponged and scratched out, and covered with a carpet of touches and

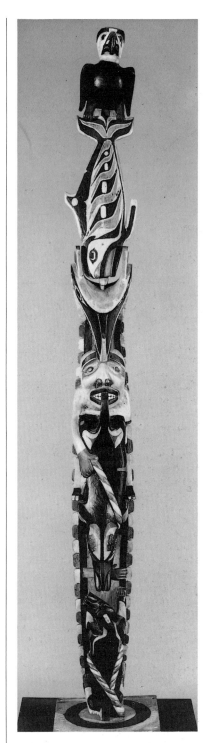

Indian gravepole from Canada

marks of every shape and size. At the very bottom, to the right, is a vigorous zig-zag reflection scrawled into the wet paint with the end of the paintbrush, and you can even see a bit of Turner's thumb-print, in a patch of the darkest paint near the bottom to the left.

Some of the ceramic and glass collection is in this room, some in a room of mixed collections next door. The collection is strong in English 18th century wares, including good glass and earthenwares. Notice the Staffordshire tea caddies and tea-pots in the shapes of a pineapple, bole of wood, and cauliflower. In contrast, bold heraldic decoration and lustrous glazes characterise the large ornamental dishes and jars made in the early 20th century by Pilkington's (not the glass giant, but a development from a smaller specialist ceramic-tile-making business). Contemporary craftspeople explore every variety of glaze, texture and weight in ceramic, for wares that may be useful, or may not. Nowhere else in the North West provides the chance to see so much work by major personalities of the business, including Janice Tchalenko (colour plate 11) and Jane Hamlyn. My favourite was Siddig El'Nigoumi's 'cross-word puzzle bowl'. The puzzle has been scratched through the top layer of ceramic in the technique called *sgraffito*. What could *1 down* be, 'He may drill you, making you study, sit up and start to talk (7)'?

The Egyptology Room is dominated by mummies, and two sections of a

J. M. W. Turner, Logging on the Upper Rhine, *watercolour*

Alison Britton, Ringed Bird, *1979*

column from the Temple of Herishef at Heracleopolis. One coffin is open, and a long dead person lies partially wrapped inside. The coffin was made for Tawuhenut, songstress of Amun, of the era 1556–1320 BC; but this is not she. The present incumbent, too long for the box, must have been put into it in some ancient economic re-use of the coffin, or more recently to ginger up an empty one for the antiquities market at the end of the last century. Other mummies are not human, but crocodile, ibis bird (most wonderfully wrapped with interleaved pleats), and falcon, all sacred companion creatures of gods. Notice on the column sections how the carvings are deeply recessed below the smooth surface, a sculptural invention of this era. We see Ramesses II, 1304–1237 BC, his name in a loop of cord that shows him as Lord of all that the Sun Encircles. Even Lords of all that the Sun Encircles, however, have to watch the budget, or so it would appear: these are second-hand columns, much older than his reign, carved with new designs to beat the drum for Ramesses. The ancient letters in this room, on sheets of crossed papyrus leaves, are curious too. It is odd how they turn the spotlight on a handful of trivial incidents, such as the use of a donkey to carry government goods to Memphis on November 30th 306 AD.

Cartonnage funerary mask from Fayum

The room opposite Egyptology shows the broadest imagineable selection of material (including some of the ceramics already mentioned). There are models of Bolton in 1838, of dinosaurs and railway engines, a selection of historic microscopes, and artefacts from non-European cultures in every corner of the world. The quality of

much of the material is very high. Indian grave poles from what is now the Canadian West dominate the centre of the room. One, from Vancouver Island, is carved with a sequence of stylised but wonderfully alive creatures: a bear at the bottom, then thunderbird, human, wolf, killer-whale, and eagle at the top. These are carvings from a culture that perceives creatures as familiar companions, not just as a food resource.

Coral Meandrina cerebriformis

Stairs from this room lead up to the Western world's attempt at something similar, a natural history museum. The displays here are straightforward and documentary, rather than theatrical, but there are plenty of specimens, all in good condition, a useful reference for enthusiasts. Birds, fish and mammals that might be seen locally are well represented. There are some exotica too. The corals are spectacular demonstrations of nature as a designer. *Gorgonia flabellum*, for example, has large, lacy, leaflike lobes, in contrast to the amazingly regular dome-shaped *Meandrina cerebriformis*. That name is not mysterious when you look at it. It is *Meandrina* because the whole surface is made up of an endless meandering ridge, fringed as a millipede is fringed with legs; and *cerebriformis* is right because the meanders resemble the convolutions of the cerebral hemispheres of the brain. Is the surface one continuous ridge, or several? Certainly there are branches, leading to dead ends, but every part I could find was connected by some mazy route to every other branch.

BURNLEY

Towneley Hall Art Gallery and Museums

Towneley Park, Burnley BB11 3RQ
(0282) 24213
Closed Saturdays. ⊞ ℗
◼ (for special bookings phone 0282 23441, Mr or Mrs Garside).
& ST: wheelchair access to ground floor only (Main Hall, Regency Rooms; *Museum of Local Crafts and Industries*; Natural History Centre); small flight of steps to lower floor.
🏛 & ⛹ welcome; phone to arrange guided visits, for which there may be a charge, except ⛹; some evening tours bookable in summer.

Many old houses have been chopped about, but not many have gone up and down like a yo-yo more often than Towneley Hall. Bits of it go back 500 years, and by the reign of Henry VIII the three wings that we now see were joined by a fourth, to enclose a courtyard. This and that was done in the 17th century, but the whole thing looked far too archaic by the early 18th century, so down came the fourth wing, in came a fancy architect and a couple of handy Swiss interior-decorators-come-plasterers, and in the last half of the 1720s much of the building was transformed. Nice modern sash windows lightened the interior, and the palazzo-type main hall in the Italian manner, as we see it today but gleaming white, replaced the dark and raftered medieval affair in which earlier Towneleys had presided over the rude mealtimes of the retainers. After five years the Swiss departed, leaving a bill for just £185.11s 4d, and modernised accommodation. Too modernised, however, for the taste of the next century. In came another fancy architect (there had been several in between, but nothing much got built), and the exterior was partially re-gothicised, with mullions for the windows, and turrets,

A. Echtler, St Mark's, Venice, *c.1880s*

though at the same time the red and blue drawing rooms were added in the Regency manner. (The architect, Jeffry Wyatt, wanted to go a lot further, and so he did when he got his hands on Windsor Castle, transmogrifying himself in the process into Sir Jeffry Wyatville.) In 1903 the Towneleys could no longer cope with their Hall, and Burnley Corporation took it over, to add to the warren of rooms and staircases the unmistakeable touches, such as doors bashed through walls, that only municipal engineers can bring to historic buildings. In short, it's a treat, and full of excellent things.

Just what the house is full of is partially explained by the history of the family. There was a Towneley at Agincourt, but the family had a couple of tough centuries after the Reformation. They remained staunchly Catholic in protestant Elizabethan and Stuart England, then staunchly Jacobite in Georgian England. Every time there was a civil war or a rebellion, Towneleys played hard for the losers, and got thoroughly clobbered. They hung onto the house, though, and proudly filled it with evidence of their faith. When Henry VIII suppressed the monasteries, a Towneley is said to have rescued from destruction the exquisite late 14th century Whalley Abbey Vestments,

which are still kept in the house. Only one other complete set of vestments is known with this kind of dense, minute stitching in silver and gold thread. Brave John Towneley, who spent twenty-five years of Elizabeth's reign imprisoned, appears in a painting of 1600 or so, old, blind and on his knees, but with his large family proudly around him, and an inscription below recording the endless transfers from gaol to gaol, and the humiliating res-

Detail of the Towneley Altarpiece

trictions imposed on his later liberty. In the family chapel (originally from the demolished early 16th century fourth wing, but carefully moved and rebuilt in its present site, panelling and all, during the modernisations) is a huge altarpiece. It is of about the same date as the original chapel, ten feet high or so, and carved with scenes of the passion, probably in Antwerp. Antwerp in those days was immensely wealthy and showy, and you would have to dive into a coral reef to find filigree more complex and delicate than the interwoven architectural forms of the canopies that frame every scene.

The altarpiece was in fact only bought in the late 18th century, by Charles Towneley. Things were getting better for English Catholics and this Towneley fitted comfortably into his age, a noted collector of classical sculptures. A particular treasure is the painting of him by Zoffany, sitting in his gallery at Westminster in 1782 with four friends, surrounded by pieces of sculpture that are now world famous. Tiresomely for Towneley, an especially choice piece, the *Discobulus*, or discus thrower, was only acquired later, and Towneley had it painted into the picture in the bottom left-hand corner, in 1792.

Apart from the splendid entrance hall, we keep coming across fine or curious rooms as we make our way up and down the staircases and along the corridors of this complicated house. There is a good kitchen, rebuilt in the Regency modernisations, fully furnished, with game hanging from the beams, shelves groaning with pewter, and the original elaborate spit over the stove. The spit must be one of the most complex surviving, and with its array of axles, rods and wheels resembles some ancient clock, enlarged as a demonstration piece. It was powered ingeniously by a vane in the chimney, turned by the hot air rising from the flames. Next door is the raftered servants' hall, where the complicated pecking order of the staff would have been jealously preserved. The Regency drawing rooms are being restored, the smaller family dining room is distinguished by unusual chevron oak panelling, and there is a fine oak gallery, with panelled bedrooms off it, now used for the special collections of furniture.

The museum collections added in this century range from prehistoric relics to contemporary art. The best of the early pictures is a large 'Tower of Babel' by the Flemish Marten van Valkenborch, a prophetic scene of frenetic activity on a vast, idiotic building project. There are four Turner watercolours, and fine Victorian paintings, including the usual sheep, forever snowbound in evening sunshine, by Farquharson, and the usual Romans, forever closeted in decadent opulence, by Alma Tadema. Good ceramics were acquired at various times, and include a T'ang bull, Lancashire 19th century slipware from Cliviger, and art nouveau ceramics, with a fine example of a vase by Walter Crane, from Pilkington's Lancastrian Pottery.

In a small room off a staircase is something unique, a room devoted to General Sir James Yorke Scarlett. You have heard about the Charge of the Light Brigade, but how about the Charge of the Heavy Brigade at the same battle? Sir James was about to

John Zoffany, Charles Towneley and Friends in the Park Street Gallery, Westminster, *1781–93*

The range in the Kitchen

retire after an impeccable peacetime military career. His time had been filled with such conscientious officer's business as the careful, lucid studies of fortifications in watercolour that we may see around the room. The Battle of Balaclava offered him one of those unmistakable moments that come once in a lifetime, and freeze lesser men into staring inaction as they pass by. At the head of 600 cavalry, he noticed that 3,000 Russian horsemen were about to descend on him from a ridge. Swiftly reforming, he led a charge on them uphill, and drove them off in eight minutes, with only twenty-eight English casualties, in the process halting the Russian advance on Balaclava. A little model in the centre of the room recreates the scene for us, though it has to be said with rather less than 3,600 participants. Unfortunately, Scarlett did not live entirely happily ever after, since he capped several more years of senior military service with an unwise charge into an unusually messy local election contest, which he lost.

CARLISLE

Carlisle Museum and Art Gallery

Tullie House, Castle Street, Carlisle,
Cumbria CA3 8TP
(0228) 34781
Closed Sundays, except during
June, July and August. ▣
& **S**: prior to redevelopment.
▥ & ♟ book in advance.
Museum will close in September
1989; new museum currently
scheduled to open in November 1990
– phone for up-to-date
information.

Carlisle's Museum and Art Gallery has
interesting collections of natural history, and of human artefacts from prehistoric times to the present. Hadrian's
Wall came right into the city, and the
collections of material from the time of
the Roman occupation are amongst the
finest in the country. The museum is
set in a quiet street on the edge of the
city centre near the cathedral, and
opposite the castle. It is situated in
Tullie House, a fine mansion of 1689
adapted for museum use in the last
century. These premises will shortly
close, for a new, specially-designed
extension is to be built, on the north
side of the complex. Currently scheduled to open in late 1990, the new

Display of Herons

Sir Edward Burne-Jones, Voyage to Vinland
the Good, *1884*

centre will present the museum's
material in totally new displays, incorporating various reconstructions and
'hands-on' exhibits; there will also be
spacious temporary exhibition galleries, and improved visitor facilities, including shop and restaurant. While the
museum is closed, look out for touring
displays on various themes, which will
be shown in local centres; activities at
the *Guildhall Museum* will also be ex-
panded during this period.

Archaeological excavations have exposed remains of Roman building in
the grounds of the present museum,
which can be seen on your way to the
entrance. The Roman collections are
currently in two ground floor rooms off
the main hallway. Hadrian gave his
wall project the go-ahead in AD 122,
and it was garrisoned until the Roman
Empire begun to curl up at the edges,
this particular edge curling up in AD
383, with the withdrawal of the garri-

son. Like the Berlin Wall, Hadrian's
was not just a wall, but a whole system
of ditches and defences. A model
makes it clear, presenting a section
through the wall, as a detail of a bird's-
eye view of the whole thing. The model
is a 1932 vintage collector's item in
itself, one of those bits of varnished
plaster and composition-work that do
not survive everywhere.

In Carlisle itself the traces of the
wall above foundation level have
vanished, but the museum's Roman
collections, mostly of objects found in
the garrison forts, provide vivid glimpses of everyday life. There are a number of altar-stones, each dedicated to
one of a whole pantheon of gods. The
votive inscriptions record the dedica-
tion to the Empire of the centurions
posted here, often from the warm
south of the Empire – Syria and Spain
– like the First Aelian Cohort of Spa-
niards, 1,000 strong, part-mounted

and keen as mustard. Their enthusiasm found an outlet, it seems, mostly in building works. We read of Marcus Aurelius Salinus, who fulfilled his vow and built a cavalry drill hall in AD 222. Smaller sacred and symbolic objects are amongst the other most interesting items. The Celtic culture in which the Romans found themselves produced, especially throughout the north west of England, strange, staring heads in stone and pottery. We have no exact idea of what they meant to their makers, but the Romans seem to have accommodated the tradition, and there is an outstanding pottery example, amongst others in stone, in this collection.

The second room is full of more everyday Roman things, found mainly in Carlisle itself. There are spoons and ladles, scrapers, and a razor. It comes as a surprise, perhaps, to find such advanced locks and keys, a bit on the large size it is true, but in metal. There are bits of a leather tent, a beautiful leather sandal with net-like uppers, and jewellery. A rare treasure is a Roman 'Filofax' – two wooden panels, each five inches by two or so, with a recessed area holding a layer of wax, into which short notes could be scratched with any pointed implement; the panels are hinged along their longest edge, so that they could be closed to protect the message.

Not many people would have known how to use the thing in the rude ages that succeeded the withdrawal of the garrison. In the corridor at present, as we leave the Roman collections, is a small but important selection of finds from burials of Vikings, six whole turbulent, uncertain centuries later. It never crossed the minds of whoever chose the 'wanted-on-voyage-through-the-afterlife' selection of grave goods buried with these warriors that they might need anything to do with namby-pamby writing. One of them had some sense of social niceties though: his comb is here, with traces of the case that protected its delicately carved teeth.

Another room on the ground floor presents the natural history of the area, especially British birds and mammals.

Most of the collection is in traditional, Victorian or Edwardian case settings. But the exhibits inside have none of the forlorn and antique look of some collections. The eagles are particularly good, one of the golden ones, the largest of English birds, compared with the smallest, a wren. For the soft hearted, there is a brown hare and a leveret. The older, didactic displays, in cases in the room's centre, are excellent, and reward a little attention with fascinating information and specimens. Where is the reproductive opening of the snail, do you suppose? – not where you think. There is poetry in the naming of parts of the mollusc: columella, body whorl, spire, umbo, and inhalent siphon. Most remarkable of all is the skeleton of a frog. It has only stumps of ribs: at first sight it seems they must have all been sheared off for some high-tech froggy heart–lung operation. But modern frogs have no ribs. They disappeared with evolution, as frogs came to breathe mainly by swallowing great gulps of air. They don't croak, they burp, which is just what it sounds like. Below the vanished rib-cage, the spine is even stranger, and very beautiful, a paperclip-thin tripod of bowed struts, to take the stress of those huge froggy leaps.

The museum has had the good fortune to receive two outstanding bequests of applied and fine art. In 1940 a Mr Williamson of Seascale left hundreds of pieces of English porcelain to the museum. He seems to have had an eye for Rococo figure groups in particular, like the candle-sticks based on Aesop's Fables (ill. on cover). Among the rarities displayed in the same gallery when I visited was a 16th century violin, not by the famous Stradivarius, but the earlier Andrea Amati, who founded the tradition of making these instruments in Cremona. There was also a footman's livery from around the turn of the 18th and 19th centuries, unusual because it is more often that special-occasion costumes of the waited-on classes survive, rather than clothes that people worked in. Carlisle's second special collection, of which parts are displayed up the grand staircase, is of English Victorian and 20th century pictures, given by Dr Gordon Bottomley and his wife. It includes a number of meticulously-detailed paintings by Arthur Hughes, and I was particularly taken by one of many studies for the poetic Dante Gabriel Rossetti's painting, 'Found', which shows a countryman in town, recognising, in a literally fallen woman,

Roman open-work shoe

his long-lost love. Good English 20th century paintings have been added over the years.

On the way up to the exhibition galleries is one surviving room, with 19th century fireplaces and panelling that imitate 17th century styles, reflecting something of the grandeur and lifestyle of the Dixon family, who once lived in Tullie House and whose portrait is on display. The room includes some cases of social history items at present.

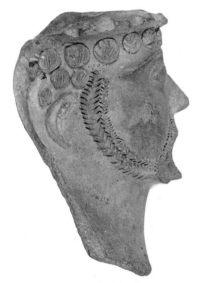

Pottery head, possibly of a Celtic deity

The museum also has a very fine collection of prehistoric material, and good geological collections; these are now in store, prior to redisplay in the new building. Among the former are extensive numbers of stone tools and weapons from thousands of years of hunter-gathering existence in these parts, including axe-heads discovered at what has been called a factory site nearby. The bronze-working cultures that followed, which were interrupted by Roman invasion, left a special treasure for Carlisle, a huge cauldron of the 1st century AD. What dainty morsels would have been ladled from its sticky depths, and for what choice company, we can only speculate.

CHESTER

Grosvenor Museum

27 Grosvenor Street, Chester
CH1 2DD   (0244) 313858
Open daily. ▣
♿ S: steps between all levels.
🚻 contact Museum Services Officer.
👥 contact Education Officer to give notice of visit, and to find out about facilities available.

Chester's Grosvenor Museum looks, from the outside, like the fruits of a hasty and unwise liaison between an Elizabethan mansion and a Loire-Valley château, delivered by a municipal midwife. Inside is a surprise – rather a grand, though odd stairwell, with a lantern at the top and with lots of quaint mosaic. Off the stairwell are galleries of fine and decorative art, of natural history, and especially of Roman antiquities. A corridor leads through to the furnished Georgian House. Returning to the main museum hall we can discover two other attractions leading from it. One is a video of the history of Chester, in a large lecture theatre. The other (sometimes occupied by temporary exhibitions) is a reassembly of the fittings from something unique to Chester, a mock Council Chamber, complete with panelling and chairs for all the officials. It was built around 1788, following a dispute as to whether the Mayor should be elected by all Freemen or just by Aldermen, and was used as a drinking and debating club. Plans for future development in the museum include a treasury of coins and silverware, and more gallery development on the upper floor level.

The Roman antiquities are in two rooms, the first of which is the recently refurbished Newstead Gallery. For the Romans, Chester was above all a fairly remote garrison near the edges of the Empire. A diorama model shows the whole Roman settlement in the sweeping Cheshire landscape. The site of the museum is easy to find, in fields be-

Joseph Smith longcase clock

tween the walls of the settlement and the river. There is also a life-size model of a legionary in armour, of the 1st century AD. As the labelling explains, defensive armour was a priority, and the centurion's shield, which looks rather like a section of a pillar-box, certainly reflects this. Even Chester's fine amphitheatre, seating 6,000, would primarily have been a *ludus* for training.

There are plenty of relics, though, of everyday life. Much revealing domestic debris, including glass and the red Samian ware used as fancy crockery throughout the Empire, turned up when archaeologists in 1976 excavated one of the wells of the inn, or *mansio*, a large building with a courtyard on the timeless pattern of inns throughout the ancient world. The well seems to have been filled after the *mansio* burned down, in the 3rd century. But not only debris had been thrown in: a skeleton, now in the display, was found there too, of a man aged about twenty whose leg had previously been broken and

Tub washing machine

improperly set. Who could he have been, this man just thrown into the well?

Most people of the time got a better send-off than the hapless hunch-leg of Chester *mansio*, and indeed legionaries had a bit more than a Denarius deducted from their annual pay as funeral insurance. The second room of Roman relics shows the results – large memorial stones, inscribed to the greater glory of the departed, and to the slightly smug satisfaction of their heirs, who paid for the stones. You did not have to be a big wheel to get a stone. One commemorates Atilianus and Anteatilianus, aged ten (twins, surely, with Anteatilianus popping out first), and Protius aged twelve. It was set up not by the parents but by Pompeius, who describes himself as their master. There are other intriguing things here too, such as the little hinged bronze inscribed plates detailing the privileges of legionaries discharged after twenty-five years service.

From here a passage leads to the Georgian House. On the way, a fine Victorian chemist's sign distinguishes the wares it lists by remarkable variation in its gilded and coloured lettering. PERSIAN ESSENCE is offered, with the promise that 'this perfume stands unrivalled'. Also amongst many

Model of a Roman legionary

wares available were medicine chests, customised for the family, the seafarer or the colonial; Oriental Tooth Paste; and horse and cattle medicines, the latter in distinctive blue lettering to keep them apart from the human ones. Further on we come to a reconstructed kitchen, and then to an array of domestic equipment. A notable specimen is the first electric washing machine made in England, a Hotpoint of 1937. An enigmatic label reveals that 'some models were also equipped with sausage-making machines'.

The furnished rooms that follow provide a setting for much of the museum's collection of pictures and decorative art. There are room settings with costumed figures from William and Mary in the 17th century to 1880 or so, with fine furniture, like the longcase clock by Chester maker Joseph Smith, in green and gold japanning, of 1730 or so. A wall case in a room of costume on the first floor also shows a unique collection of recorders, including a complete set of four, by the late 17th century maker Pierre Bresson; the museum shop sells a record to give an idea of how they sound.

More fine and decorative art is displayed in a luxuriously refurbished gallery, opened in February 1989, at the top of the main staircase. Amongst the best paintings, George Barret's picture of the ruins of nearby Beeston Castle is a quite rare opportunity to see a painting of this period still in something like the condition in which it left the artist's studio. It shows how much cool colouring there was originally in many pictures, which we have got used to as warm old brown things because of the accumulation of dirt, and deterioration of varnish and paint. Note the figures in this picture, which are of the kind

Henry Pether, Chester Castle by Moonlight, *1853–61*

known to art historians as staffage, stock characters to fit the mood. There is always a bare-footed rustic, like the one in the foreground group here, fine in Italy, perhaps, but surely not very idyllic in Cheshire; and is it not rude of the gentry always to be pointing, like the well-dressed figure to the right, being shown the ruins by a guide?

The natural history is in the Kingsley gallery, half way up the main staircase. Not all the cases in this room present the last word in museum display, but they are informative, with good specimens. There are fine fossils, including an ammonite, a giant spiral-shelled tentacled sea-dweller, within the whorls of whose shells magnificent casts of sediment fossilised. Amongst the mammals note the extraordinary gesture and expression of the hare. The butterflies and moths have been effectively redisplayed in a way that is colourful as well as instructive. They are especially good on camouflage and mimicry. It is hard indeed to make out the Dusky Knot-grass Dagger Moth on a bit of lichen. Amongst the mimics, the Narrow Bordered Bee-Hawk moth looks just like a bumble-bee. Its wings have lost all their scales, and become transparent. The gorgeous Peacock butterfly is making fierce eyes at everyone. Most cunning of all is the Chinese Character Moth, *Cilix glaucata*, which looks just like a bit of bird-dropping. It's a tough life, being a butterfly or a moth, and you have to bluff your way to survive, whether by showing off or by going around looking like ****.

Wax jack

ELLESMERE PORT

The Boat Museum

The Boat Museum Trust, Dockyard Road, Ellesmere Port, South Wirral L65 4EF   (051) 355 5017
Closed Fridays November to March. 🅰 (additional charges for boat trips). ▣ 🅿
♿ **AT**: most of museum accessible to
disabled visitors; lifts to upper floors; fairly large site.
🏨 & 🚻 contact Education Service for details of charges, services and booking arrangements. ◎

Some 'industrial heritage' museums glamourise the past, but not the Boat Museum. True, there is one display entitled 'Ellesmere Port, a nostalgic history', but even this turns out to be unsentimental, and excellently researched. The siting of the museum on the Mersey estuary rules out a rose-tinted view of things. Just downstream giant containers are hoisted through the air by the huge yellow gantries of a container port, while upstream is a series of petro-chemical installations. All the

same, a visit to the Boat Museum is like a trip to the seaside. It is a place where the sky and water meet in dramatic horizons in many directions, as you wend your way along quays and over bridges, climbing into brightly-painted barges, discovering the many excellent documentary displays or setting off on a boat trip. Visit on a sunny day if possible, to benefit from the play of light on the water pouring through sluices, trapped in small basins, or spread out, with the breeze sweeping across it, in large ones.

The displays are very varied, and in

View of the Boat Museum

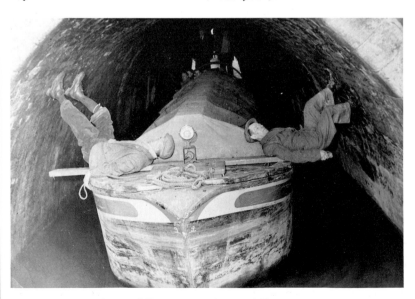

Two men legging through a tunnel, Trent & Mersey Canal, c.1965

The kitchen range in the cottage of about 1900, Porters Row

Class of Schoolboys, Ellesmere Port, c.1910

section on tunnels, you can see how men lay on their backs and 'walked' the barges along with their feet on the tunnel roof. There are convincing reconstructions of workshops. The rope workshop is unusual, with huge knotted masses of rope as beautiful as sculptures. The ropes did not just have to be strong enough to pull the barges along, but to slow them down too, thrown around bollards on the approach to the locks so that the friction of the rope around the bollard took the strain. With time the bollards became eroded into particular shapes, like rocks carved and polished by the tide. You can sit in a narrowboat in this display, and watch a video of the history of the canals as a means of transport. In the building next door two Armstrong steam-driven pumps that supplied hydraulic power to the docks can be seen, sometimes working. In other buildings you can come across a blacksmith's forge, where commissions are taken; a working stable, since horses were a great part of the life of the canals; and workshops, where a variety of contemporary craftspeople have businesses.

On the far side of the site from the entrance is Porters Row, a short street of cottages. There used to be twelve of them, built for £780 in 1833. On a hoarding at the end of the street a replica advertisement exhorts us to use Sunlight Soap if we long for 'the luxury of a clean shirt'. Inside the cottages, the ground floors have been fitted out to show the lifestyles of the 1840s, 1900 or so, the 1930s, and the 1950s. 1840 is very sparse, but, as the caption says, would have been regarded as good accommodation for a working family at the time. By the 1950s it is all more familiar, with even a television, showing broadcasts of the period, such as Anthony Eden complaining about Colonel Nasser. In the 1900 cottage you may find a fire in the grate of the range, washing hanging up to dry, and there to greet you the lady of the house in a period dress. This is no actress, but someone who knows enough of living in such a house to black-lead the range every week, and instruct the blacksmiths how to make missing or

most of the buildings on the site you will discover something relating to the history of the town, or of the canals and the workings of the dock. The main display is over the locks from the ticket office, in the island Warehouse. Photo-

graphs testify to a hard life. In the section 'Life in the country', five children, six adults (one of them a woman smoking a pipe), and a dog camp out in front of a mere scrap of canvas thrown over tied sticks for a shelter. In the

View of the Ropemaker's shop

GRASMERE

Dove Cottage

and

The Grasmere and Wordsworth Museum

The Wordsworth Trust, Centre for British Romanticism, Dove Cottage, Grasmere, Cumbria LA22 9SH
(09665) 544/547
Open daily. 🚻 ▣ 🅿
🚹 S: limited.
🚻 & 🚻 phone to give notice of visit and for information of special facilities available.

Wordsworth's sister, Dorothy, noted in her journals that when her brother and his household set themselves up in Dove Cottage, only a couple of carts went by a week, and a carriage was not seen in years. Things are not quite like that any more in Grasmere, but all the same it remains an extremely beautiful site, in the middle of a broad valley in

A lock of Wordsworth's hair

worn parts for it. Do not fail to view the outside lavatory either, where a surprise awaits you.

But of course the stars of the museum are the boats (colour plate 13). They were not just transporters for goods, but floating homes as well, for the families who made a livelihood for themselves and their horses on the canals. You can explore 'Friendship' in the indoor comfort of the main display, or wander round the quays outside to discover 'Puppis' and 'Merak', Merope' and 'Scorpio', and many others. Climb aboard, with just a little agility, and explore their cabins. There was not an inch to be wasted, and the woodwork is a magic world of little drawers, cupboards and shelves, decorated with brilliantly-coloured painted flowers and landscapes. Usually there was also some brass-work, lace edgings to shelves and beams, and a lot of crockery. Outside, the boats are even more boldly decorated than inside.

The Boat Museum got underway in the late 1970s, thanks in particular to a great deal of voluntary work by local people and canal enthusiasts. Their efforts were exactly in the right place at the right time to attract a good deal of government cash, in the wake of the Toxteth riots. The mixture of enthusiasm and resources now offers an unusually convincing museum.

the heart of the Lake District. There are two parts to your museum visit here. The Wordsworth Museum has one of the finest collections of literary manuscripts in the world, and uses them, along with mementoes, to present the life of Wordsworth and his circle; there is also a space for temporary exhibitions, on related themes. A few yards up the road is the white-washed Dove Cottage, into whose tiny rooms the ever-growing household was packed, and which can be visited on a guided tour.

Artists rather than poets first discovered the Lake District as a place worthy to spend time in for persons of sense and sensibility. The first room of the museum, to the right as we enter, chronicles their discovery. Nobody would have come to such a desolate spot before the 18th century if they did not have to, but by the time the lowlands of England had been mostly cleared of forest, people began to discover that there was something enticing about wild places after all. Trim fields are all very well, but they are not the kind of places where you can commune with your ancestors. Broad valleys, craggy mountains and crashing waterfalls are on a grander scale, and that is how they are represented in the prints and paintings on display. We can watch the romantic pressure rising in the pictures on show, as the familiar forms of land and lake disappear beneath ever more looming masses of cloud, lightened by courageous early attempts at painting rainbows.

You did not even have to paint to join in. You could set off to see famous views (and woe betide the landowner with a cracking good waterfall on his estate who did not set up observation spots and shelters for the gentry) with a Claude glass, like the one on display in the showcase here. It is a small curved mirror, just about the size of a wing mirror, and giving a similarly reduced view, but in deeply darkened glass, which drained the view of most colour. The great thing was to find a bit of nature offering a combination of mountains and trees reminiscent of the works of the 17th century French painter, Claude. Then you turned your

Letter from William and Dorothy Wordsworth to Samuel Coleridge

Wordsworth's ice skates

he or she fixed the other eye on a sheet of paper, so that the view seen via the mirror could be mentally superimposed for tracing onto the blank sheet. This device is connected, too, with the history of photography. It was so hard to use that the English photographic pioneer, Henry Fox Talbot, invented his process out of sheer frustration at failing to draw with one.

Upstairs, there is first a reconstruction of a Lake District statesman's kitchen-cum-living room. Then comes a display of decorated eggs by James Dixon, a servant of the Wordsworths for thirty years, whose talents in the egg-painting line so moved Queen Victoria that she sent him five pounds. The two long rooms that follow are the heart of the museum, presenting the lives of Wordsworth and his circle. His birth at ten o'clock at night is recorded in the family bible. A list of books forwarded to him after his father's death suggests no particular literary background: one novel, a run of a periodical, a little mathematics, some law books and, of course, some sermons. There are drafts of poems, including some for the autobiographical *Prelude*, one of which shows one line of the page struck vigorously through, the rest without a correction. One touching document has to be shown in reproduction: Wordsworth had an illegitimate child by a French girl, Annette Vallon, whilst travelling in France as a very young man, during the French Revolution; her letter to Wordsworth after war had separated them survives because the gendarmerie, not Wordsworth, received it. By the time a break in the Napoleonic Wars put the two back in touch a decade later, in 1802, Wordsworth was engaged to a friend from boyhood, Mary Hutchinson. A more entertaining correspondence shows Wordsworth reluctant to be involved in an English edition of the French fairytale, '*La Belle et La Bête*' (Beauty and the Beast): 'I confess there is something disgusting in the notion of a human being consenting to *mate* with a beast, however aimiable his qualities of heart.'

There are headphones that visitors can raise to hear recitations of poetry in

back on it, and looked at the view reflected in your little mirror, moving it to and fro until you got as near as you could to a Claude composition, and fainted with pleasure.

Persons who were able to keep a steady hand through all this could try to use one of the other aids displayed here to draw with. The simplest is the ancestor of the photographic camera, the 'camera obscura'. Where the film would now be, the artist simply put a sheet of translucent paper, on which to trace the outlines of the picture projected by the lens. More difficult to use was the 'camera lucida', also displayed. A little periscope affair reflected the view into one of the artist's eyes, whilst this room and the next, which follows Wordsworth's life from his meeting with Samuel Taylor Coleridge in 1795. A bit short of cash, the two set to work on the *Lyrical Ballads*, Wordsworth's contributions intended to imbue the everyday with the intensity of the supernatural, Coleridge's including *The Ryme of the Ancient Mariner*, aiming to make the supernatural as real as the everyday. There are traces of the everyday Wordsworth here too: his inkstand, his spectacles, tinted spectacles, cloak and waistcoat, his socks with 'WW' embroidered on them, his walking-stick, panama hat and umbrella. There are also mementoes of special days, skates for frozen ones, and most special of all the court suit for the day on which he was presented to Queen Victoria as Poet Laureate (Tennyson wore the same coat when it came to his turn). Amongst the manuscripts is the complete transcript of Wordsworth's poetry, prepared by Dorothy and Mary Wordsworth for Coleridge to take with him when he left for Italy in 1804, for the sake of his health.

The Wordsworths lived at Dove Cottage from 1799 to 1808. Thanks to a legacy, Wordsworth had an income of a few tens of pounds a year, but was not wealthy at a time when a young couple with aspirations needed £150 or so a year for a town house with a maid. Life must have been pretty basic, with the

Plant book and microscope owned by Wordsworth

Wordsworth's spectacles and case

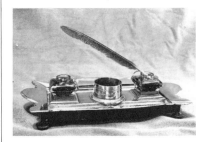

Wordsworth's inkstand and a quill

nearest water in a pump some 100 yards away. The cottage would not have been over large for William, his wife Mary and sister Dorothy; but then there were children too, and with Coleridge, De Quincey, and their friends and children, there were often between ten and twenty people living here. Perhaps the initials embroidered on Wordsworth's socks bear witness to one of life's minor struggles in such a mêlée. The Wordsworths' bedroom is so small that there would be no room for today's visitors had their bed, tiny though it is, been left in it (the bed can now be seen upstairs). People were smaller then, but even so, the Wordsworths must have been fond of one another to survive in such a small bed. All the furniture is of extreme simplicity, including a clock that Wordsworth bought for seven shillings in Kendal market. If he wanted to escape from all this, he took just the tiny portmanteau we see here, setting out for months of travel with one change of clothing and a notebook. There is the guest room to see as well, where Sir Walter Scott and De Quincey would have slept, the children's room, which Dorothy lined with newspaper to try to keep out the damp, and the delightful garden, rising steeply up behind the cottage (colour plate 9).

HELMSHORE

Helmshore Textile Museums

Holcombe Road, Helmshore, Rossendale, Lancashire BB4 4NP
(0706) 226459
Open daily March to October, and only on Sunday afternoons November to February. 🚉 ▣ 🅿
♿ W: except for upper floors of Higher Mill, which are inaccessible to wheelchair-bound; if bringing a group of disabled phone in advance.
🚻 & 🚻 phone in advance to give notice and for information about special facilities (e.g. a guide); out-of-hours group visits can usually be arranged throughout the year.

The museums of the Lancashire textile industry at Helmshore are housed in two adjoining mills. Higher Mill finished woollen cloth, turning it into a heavy blanket-like material by the process of fulling, until 1967. Whittakers Mill processed waste from the surrounding cotton industry into thread,

Reconstructed bobbin-making shop

Exterior view of Higher Mill, a water-powered fulling mill built in 1789

Fulling stocks and waterwheel inside Higher Mill

workshops that turned out parts for the machinery. Early textile machines depended on relatively little metal and much wood, held together with string and leather. Working at any speed, they must have required the most subtle settings of play and tension at every joint, to keep them going without breaking thread or knocking themselves to pieces. A world of ingenious, often tiny parts kept the show on the road, with a jargon of specialist terms. We can see how they made the healds – twisted loops of wire that guided the long warp threads, or reeds, like huge combs, keeping hundreds of threads at a time separate – and many other parts. The six stages in making the sleek shuttles, which on automatic machines fly to and fro almost too fast for the eye to catch them, culminate in the fixing of the sharp steel tips that make it best not to stand in line with them in working demonstrations: they occasionally fly from the looms. There is a wholesaler's display case of parts from a Rochdale factory of the 1920s, with mule underclearer clips, buffer spiral springs, taper bow springs, weavers' nippers and no.18 travellers, and dozens more.

As a reminder that there were people in the middle of all this, there is the brightly chromo-lithographed certificate recording the membership in 1885 of James Edward Morris in the Amalgamated Association of Card and Blowing Room Operatives. Every possible space has been filled with some righteous exhortation to toil on with obedient diligence. 'Honest labour bears a lovely face', it says, and 'Labour shall refresh itself with Hope.' Better still: 'Let us then be up and doing, / with a heart for any fate, / still achieving, still pursuing, / learn to labour and to wait.' Terrific! No welfare state nonsense about that; a day's work was a day's work in those days. Just a touch heavy on the waiting and hoping bit? Whose side was this association on?

A chronological visit to the larger machinery would begin with the fulling process, at the back of Higher Mill. The stream powering the mill runs alongside, and the sound of running

until 1978. Much original machinery for the two processes is still on site, in working order. In addition, important related equipment has been collected, and there are ample documentary displays. Best of all, you can talk here to people who worked in the industry and now demonstrate the machinery, bringing it all alive from years of real experience.

A visit begins in a zig-zag corridor with documentary displays about the industries, enlivened with reconstructions of some of the myriad specialist water is constant here. A grand water-wheel revolves sedately at one end of a stone-floored, raftered room. It turns an iron axle, fitted with tappetted wheels, which used to trip the ten man-sized wooden hammers in a row running the length of the room. They look as if they would wake the dead when working, but one of them can still be seen and heard at work, electrically powered, and it makes only a dull thud at the end of its two-foot drop. The room is filled almost restfully with the sloshing of water, and the creak of timber. The hammers, aided by the effect of soap produced from the lanolin in the wool, shrank and matted the fabric, turning it into a thick, heavy woollen cloth.

Upstairs in Higher Mill are early spinning machines for the cotton industry. Spinning was the bottleneck of the business: eight or so spinners, using cottage spinning wheels, were required to keep one weaver busy, even one using only a hand-operated loom. This was a golden opportunity for entrepreneurs, and machines here show how it was seized, especially by Hargreaves of the spinning jenny, and Arkwright of the water frame and much else. Their machines look like daft contraptions, but they affected the lives of millions for better or worse.

Retracing our steps to Whittakers Mill we can see the fully-industrialised solutions to the thread question found by the end of the last century. This mill used not raw cotton, but short waste fibres (the ones that did not get into the workers' lungs!), which were the in-

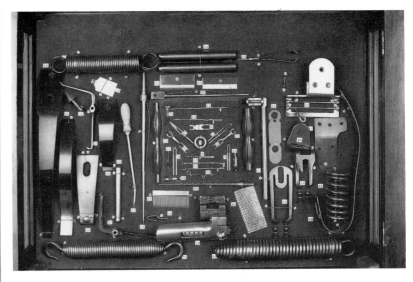

Some of the metal machine parts available from Nuttalls of Rochdale, c.1920

evitable by-product of the cotton industry. A long room of machinery processed the raw waste, in machines like the Jumbo, for loosening up hard waste, and the Devil, which ripped it to shreds with spiked wheels spinning at 800 rpm. The Devil tended to take operators' fingers off too, regularly set its cotton alight, and lived in a Devil-Hole. The end product of this room was a forty-six inch wide, softly felted roll of evenly mixed fibres, called the lap, for feeding to the thread-making process.

Upstairs, an expert operates spinning machinery, and explains the many stages in the process. The big machines look clumsy but are dextrous, rubbing rows of thread between oscillating aprons of castor-oil lubricated leather, twisting and stretching the yarns to just the right tension. Cloud-like ropes of tenuously linked fibres are teased from the edge of the initial lap roll, then combined, eighty-eight soft ropes at a time, into one, for processing into a thin, loosely-twisted thread called roving, which is given to the mules for spinning. The mules spin cotton onto a total of 1,428 spindles at a time. A long armature almost the length of the room, on dainty wheels running on short rails, runs five foot or so back-

wards to draw, twist and stretch thread from 714 spools at a time. The whirring stops, a long rail lifts the thread to re-route it, and as the armature rolls back the finished threads are wound onto the spindles. The machines wind miles of thread as they roll to and fro, four times each minute. Two men would have kept these machines on the go, walking twenty miles a day on the watch for broken threads, in bare feet, so that they could pick the threads up with their toes, rather than bend hundreds of times a day. Breaks were joined by the merest twist of the fingers, a skill that took years to perfect. Woe betide the apprentice who held things up whilst learning. This was piece-work, and as your demonstrator may recall, there was nothing to deter a mean overseer from hitting a beginner who cost him wages.

At the end of the room are the offices, with machines for testing the quality of the thread. On the wall hangs another framed exhortation, this time for the managerial classes: 'Call upon a man of Business in Business hours only on Business, and go about your Business in order to give him time to finish his Business.' No time for time-consuming time-management courses at that time.

Demonstrator at a spinning mule

KENDAL

Abbot Hall

Kendal, Cumbria LA9 5AL
(0539) 22464
Closed on Sunday mornings, and
on Saturday mornings 1 November
to Spring Bank Holiday. 🅱 🅿
🚻 **S**: lift to first floor; improved
access, including ramps, scheduled
for completion 1991.
🚻 & 🚻 phone the Director or
Keeper of Paintings to book, and
for information about worksheets
for 🚻 ; reduced party rates if pre-
booked.

Kendal must have a lot of clout as well
as style to have put together as good a
collection as they now display, in a
building opened as a gallery only as
recently as 1962. The present Georgian Abbot Hall is on the site of a
medieval abbot's hall, once the property of St Mary's Abbey, York. After the
dissolution of the monasteries, a long
succession of lay owners bought or
inherited the hall. One of them rebuilt
it, at the end of the 1750s, reputedly
with the help of the distinguished
northern architect, John Carr of York.
It remains a fine house, its ground
floor rooms restored to an 18th century
appearance. From its fine panelled and
pillared rooms, bow windows look out
on to lawns leading down to the river.

From the entrance, visitors may turn
right into a small staircase hall, containing paintings that are changed on a
regular basis. The room beyond contains some of the treasures of the
collection, by the 18th century portrait-
ist, George Romney, a Lakeland man
by origin. In the 1920s he had a greater
reputation than he has now, but Abbot
Hall's collection shows him at his best.
His early portraits show trim figures in
everyday dress represented in unpre-
tentious interiors and landscapes, in a
style of jewel-like clarity. The likeness
of Captain Robert Banks is a fine
portrait of this kind. The captain's was
later to be abandoned to a servant by

George Romney, The Gower Family, *1776*

John Ruskin, Study of rocks and ferns in a wood
at Crossmount, Perthshire, *1847*

The Dining Room at Abbot Hall

the family, who knew the painter just as a local joiner with a little extra talent. A portrait of the artist's brother, James, aged ten, painted in 1761, recalls the kind of old master paintings that Romney would have managed to look at. It shows the little boy holding a candle, the light shining around and through his fingers, an effect that had earlier made a living for the Dutch painter, Gottfried Schalcken, in particular.

Romney's later manner is very different: blurry, atmospheric, and, in the required manner of portraiture for the polite classes later in the 18th century, full of allusions to classical taste. The large 'Gower Family' shows how well Romney at his best could do this kind of thing. It is not, frankly, a picture with whose mood most of us can feel comfortable today. Knowing that the children are the Lady Susan, the Lady Georgiana, the Hon Granville, the lady

Charlotte Leverson-Gower and, with the tambourine, the Lady Anne, does not help either in bringing it all much closer to the average home. It helps to see it as a bit of dressing-up, and to work out that it depends on a clever compositional trick, which plays upon visual perception. The centre of the picture is empty, except for joined hands, which complete a dancing ring, with three children grouped to the left, and one isolated on the right. Behind the girl on the right is an older one, with a tambourine. The eye, instinctively trying to divide the figures into groups, first associates the isolated dancer with the other children in the ring, then pairs her with the tall figure behind her on the right. The uncertainty makes it impossible for the figures to look as if they are in static groups, and helps us to catch the mood of the dancing figures. Notice, too, that

under his curls and draperies the young Hon Granville looks as streetwise as an alley-cat.

Nearby is a contrast: a fine dolls' house, in the typical early form of a simple box, divided into rooms. Dolls' houses are often worth very careful scrutiny indeed, for anyone with an eye for the bizarre. Such strange things turn out to be going on, given even a touch of imagination. This one does not disappoint at all. Look at the maid coming down the stairs. She holds a brush, of the dust-pan-and-brush variety, but of colossal proportions: the hairs would be two foot long. It looks like something from a dream just beginning to go bad on you, and a glance in the room upstairs turns the corner. This is one for Professor Freud all right. The lady on the sofa has a doll beside her; it is obviously a representation of some man in her life, her husband perhaps, shrivelled by fantasy or magic to tiny proportions. Look, he has no hands or feet, though his legs are minutely articulated, and one whole shin is missing. Notice that she allows her dog to threaten him humiliatingly, but teasingly preserves him from harm; her dog has no front legs at all.

Detail of embroidered box, c.1655–60

The other rooms on the ground floor of the real house contain many treasures. The furniture is very fine, much of it by the Lancaster firm of Gillows, and the wall cabinets are full of varied surprises. Look out for a T'ang ceramic horse from 9th century China, or the wonderful pedlar doll of 1820 or so. She has not just the usual basket of goods, but a three-decker stand with mirrors, and every kind of domestic trinket, incredibly miniaturised. When you find her, notice alongside the much earlier silk-embroidered casket. Dating from the mid-17th century, it is unusually well preserved, a feast of specialised stitchery in glowing colours, with a representation of sheep-shearing on the lid.

The last room on the ground floor contains a wonderful giant Turner watercolour, one of the tall, dark views into Alpine ravines with misty blue depths, which he painted in 1805. The great Victorian theorist, John Ruskin, adored these paintings, and the room is full of an unusually good collection of his own greatly under-rated watercolours, which indicate why he admired Turner's so much. One shows the most intricate attention to rock forms, of the kind suggested in the aforementioned Turner. Another, 'Near Interlaken', is all atmosphere, with sunshine on a hilltop masked by a shaded ridge. There are studies of the fine detail of feathers, too, but the painting that best shows Ruskin's range is a 'Study of Rocks and Ferns'. Look at the amazing texture, shape and detail of the trunk of the birch tree, then at the hard wiry edges in other parts of the picture, where pools of free, wet watercolour have been hastily put in, then boldly left alone to dry untouched. They perfectly represent the parts of this immensely complex subject. You can see more of Ruskin's work in his house at *Brantwood*, of course, on the lakeside just outside Coniston.

Upstairs, the rooms are either devoted to temporary exhibitions, or to Abbot Hall's 20th century collection. This, too, is of special quality, with good pieces by Ben Nicholson and Arp, and a rare collection of the work of the German, Kurt Schwitters, who settled here to make his constructions – odd at first, but very beautiful when you get the hang of them. If exhibitions mean that all these works are not on show, at least you can see a Barbara Hepworth sculpture in the courtyard in front of the Hall.

1989 sees the beginning of a major capital building scheme at Abbot Hall, which will result in more display space on the first floor, thus ensuring that part of the contemporary art collection is always on display. Work should be completed in 1991.

Kendal Museum of Natural History and Archaeology

Station Road, Kendal, Cumbria LA9 6BT   (0539) 21374
Closed Sunday mornings, and on Saturday mornings 1 November to Spring Bank Holiday. 🛗🅿
♿: wheelchair access to all galleries by prior appointment.
🚻 & 🚻 phone Education Officer to book, and for details of services available.

Kendal Museum has local history collections of the kind that many local museums have, illuminating and touching, but not extraordinary. Its natural history collections, however,

are extraordinary. What is more, they have recently been redisplayed in an exceptionally interesting and imaginative way, to explain how species depend on the environment they live in, and on one another. The museum's huge collection of birds is also available for enthusiasts and specialists to study, but this is behind the scenes, and by appointment.

A visit might begin with the local history, on the ground floor. Life in this area was characterised for many centuries by conflict with raiders from what is now Scotland; hence the number of finds in the display from nearby Roman forts, and odd relics of the 'Forty Five' (the Jacobite 1745 rebellion). Amongst the remnants of the extensive Roman presence are memorial stone altars, a delicate leather shoe, and a hoard of coins of the late 4th century. There is nothing unusual in

Detail of the Roman Food display

Woodland scene in the Natural History gallery

the burial of such a hoard in troubled times, just as the protective power of Rome was retreating, but nobody knows even where this hoard was buried; it was found, not in the ground, but in the museum stores, a few years ago. A more unusual hoard is one of unused Roman-period iron nails. Such things represented advanced technology for the time, and these were buried deliberately, to prevent invaders getting them when a fort was abandoned. Now they are arranged, eleven of them from two to about ten inches long, unspoiled by use. Metalwork was strong in the area, and there are beautiful 'Dragonesque' bronze brooches, and an iron 'hipposandal' – an iron plate that could be fastened to a horse's hoof for work on hard roads (the shoeing of horses had not been introduced at the time).

There is another hoard later on, this one also from troubled times – the Wars of the Roses, with coins of Edward III, Edward IV, and Richard III, of evil or maligned memory, depending on your point of view. Kendal was less troubled by war in these centuries, but the usual dismal evidence of violence and coercion, even in a small town, is

here. Notably grim is a 'scold's bridle', or 'branck', an iron frame that fitted over the head and forced a metal tongue into the victim's mouth, just over his or her own tongue, but serrated, to discourage speech. Thumbscrews were routine law-enforcement issue up here too, it seems. Peaceful citizens got on with making implements out of horn. A curious set of six pieces on display shows the stages in making a spoon out of a cow's horn. The first item is natural horn, the second shows how it was roughly sawn, to leave a crude handle and scoop shape. The secret ingredient was heating, which made the horn malleable, so that it could be opened out for final shaping and polishing.

Upstairs is the first of the natural history galleries, devoted to the evolution of the Lake District and its inhabitants. This part of the earth's crust has been, at one time or another over the last 500 million years, desert and even shallow sea. Exquisite fossils, lit to show off the delicacy with which their original forms have been preserved as stone replaced tissue, particle by particle, chronicle the changing environment. Most of the room, though, is

devoted to the Lake District environment today. Circular windows provide glimpses of every kind of habitat, amongst them a roadside verge, an estuary, a limestone wood, a Kendal back garden, and underwater Windermere. At the back of each of these recent displays is a backdrop, by Lynn Denman, who paints with great skill, mixing a scientific eye for landforms with plenty of feeling. It comes as a surprise to see how different these habitats are, and how specific to each their inhabitants. They are animated by a host of creatures – squirrels, moles, sparrowhawks and an evil-looking pike. In a sad case of its own is the one-week-old kid of a roe deer, no more than a few inches long. It died after its mother abandoned it, and incidentally makes the point that creatures are never killed nowadays for displays like this, which depend instead on road accident casualties and specimens found by chance, in good condition.

That was not at all the case with many of the larger exotic mammals in Kendal's collection, felled in the days of unrestrained big-game hunting by Colonel E.G. Harrison, who presented his collections to the museum. A little plaque shows off some of the huge, grotesquely deformed lead bullets recovered from the bodies of several of his victims. Old photographs of the museum show the Colonel's trophies displayed in the usual dismal arrays. Now they are used in a room devoted to showing the world as a single, delicate natural system, which we are

'From a Kendal Window' display

destroying. A display of processes in the top few inches of soil familiar to everyone explains the point, and the gorilla, baby elephant, towering polar-bear, and many other creatures help to extend it to a world scale.

There is a particularly telling intro-duction, about evolution. The skeletons of a wolf and a dolphin show how species at first glance quite diffe-rent can be related bone by bone, though the shapes of each bone have been drastically transformed as the lines of evolution diverged. No one knows how evolution works, but Dar-win's version can be shown to play a part, even if not to explain everything. The local peppered moth makes the point. On the lichen-covered tree-trunks of unpolluted, pre-industrial England, versions of these moths with a dusting of brown on grey colouring were almost invisible; rare, dark-brown variants were soon spotted by pre-dators. But now, in polluted areas, it is the dark variants, called *Carbonaria*, that dominate. For lichens no longer lighten the dark tree-trunks there, and it is the pale, dusted moths that get eaten before they breed. Two speci-mens of tree-trunk, one lichen-covered and one not, each with a pale and a dark moth, demonstrate how effectively their camouflage matches the alternative conditions. Displays of wonderfully exotic birds from Kendal's special collection show how inventive is evolution. Perhaps the birds of Tanza-nia and Zambia win on colour, but surely the Eastern-Australian Lyre Bird gets the prize for imagination; the three-dimensional whorls and spirals of feather it displays make peacocks look crude.

The information in these thought-provoking displays is never overdone, but for those wanting more, there is a video in the lower gallery, and an audio-visual programme about Lake-land life in the upper gallery. Mystery objects on a shelf at the back of that gallery can be picked up for examina-tion. They are all things you might come across on a lakeland ramble, and when you have guessed what they might be, there is a concealed list of answers to check with.

Museum of Lakeland Life and Industry

Abbot Hall, Kendal, Cumbria
LA9 5AL   (0539) 22464
Closed on Sunday mornings, and on Saturday mornings 1 November to Spring Bank Holiday. 🚻 🅿
♿ **S**: wheelchair access to ground floor and Farm Barn only.
🚹 & 🚺 phone the Director of this Museum to book, and for information about services available.

We 'off-comers', as visitors to the lakes are called, may associate the area with leisure, but the Museum of Lakeland Life is above all a museum of Lakeland work. Few museums manage to pack in displays of quite so many trades, and in case you think they have missed the vital business of farming, do not fail to find the Farm Barn, a whole gallery devoted to the subject, set apart from the other displays, off the Craft Shop. It is not all-work-and-no-play, how-ever: there is sport in the form of the Lakes' speciality of wrestling, and the Grasmere Guides Race (compared with which, the display suggests, mere fell-running is an amateurish busi-ness). There are also lots of details of domestic life. Finally, there is a room devoted to the author of children's Lakeland adventure yarns, Arthur Ransome.

Printing comes first, with a fine press, and amongst the fittings from a jobbing printers a case of the giant wooden blocks that were used for the big lettering, inches high but very thin, on posters of the kind seen in westerns. Then comes weaving, since Kendal had a thriving woollen industry before the industrial revolution. Besides a large loom and a spinning wheel, there is a small treasure here, a cloth measuring rod of about 1500, with a capped head and intricate carvings along its length.

Next is a rest from labour, in the form of a reconstruction of a late 19th century living room. Remarkable amongst the furnishings are an espe-cially splendid gramophone, for cylin-ders, not discs, and a cabinet full of grottoes made out of crystals, en-

The Chemist's shop in Queensgate

Newspaper boy in the printing display

hanced by mirrors. Just as a reminder that home is a workplace as well, the staircase that follows is decorated with domestic appliances. Here are several washing machines, from the simple plunger type to one of the labour-saving wooden ones, with a big handle to turn the washing around, and several vacuum cleaners too. The bellows-operated Torst, we are assured by its manufacturer's label, was pre-eminent, but it must have been harder work than the electric Goblin beside it.

At the top of the stairs you enter a mid-18th century kitchen, full of local oak furniture. A maid slaves over the hearth at her mistress's command. Hams, salmon, trout, cheese, fruit and vegetables show the range of food then eaten. Typical 18th century recipes are displayed. Then it is on to the bed-room, dominated by a large and ornately carved oak four-poster bed, with pretty patchwork bedspread, and beyond it to displays of costume and jewellery. There are two cases of fine jewellery, one of them full of stunning black mourning pieces, made out of jet and its substitutes. Real jet is fossilised wood; amongst the imitations are items made of vulcanite, which is rubber treated with sulphur and heated to

harden it, in which state the material could be carved or moulded.

Across a landing over the centre of the stable-block, and it is back to work with a vengeance. Past a blacksmith's forge and a turn-of-the-century mechanic's workspace (colour plate 12), the latter with a full set of the tools that show how versatile and know-ledgeable these general engineers had to be, we come to a joiner's and wheel-wright's shop, and then to house-painters' and coachpainters' equip-ment. Notice the numerous planes for mouldings, rare indeed now, and the varnish-encrusted door, like a coral-covered relic of a shipwreck, on which the coach painter was in the habit of cleaning his brushes. Next is a display about the clogs for which the North is famous, and which were indeed indis-pensable for work in wet, dangerous conditions. Only the soles were of carved wood; the uppers were leather, and metal strengtheners were added where the conditions of one trade or another required them. The huge knives that the clogger used to cut out the soles are here, jointed to the bench so that the three-foot-long handles act as levers to slice the curving six inch blades through the wood. Finally, after a grinding and buffing machine fitted with a grand array of abrasive and polishing wheels, comes one of the machines that turned out the endless stream of bobbins wanted for the cot-ton industry, with a central spindle that revolved at 6,000 rpm.

Down a passage lined with toys, a toyshop to the right, and dolls to right and left, is a room devoted to Arthur Ransome, author of *Swallows and Ama-zons* and similar gripping Lakeland boating adventures of the 1930s. On the left are photographs and photo-copies of notable manuscripts, and on the right a desk that he inherited from his father, laden with some of his possessions. Perhaps he was a bit of a traditionalist. There are eighteen of his pipes here, and a jar of the dip-pen nibs that he stuck to, spurning the new-fangled fountain pens, though he did use the splendid Imperial type-writer here. He was no stranger to real adventure, having been in Russia dur-

ing the Revolution, where he met, and later married as his second wife, Trots-ky's private secretary. On the desk are his miniature travelling candlesticks, vital to enable him to read and write during the long train journeys with which he threaded Russia in the pur-suit of his research into fairytales and folk stories.

A narrow flight of stairs leads to two rooms containing furniture by the Kendal maker, Arthur Simpson, and glorious fabrics by Annie Garnett, two of the mainstays of the Arts and Crafts Movement inspired by the writings and philosophy of John Ruskin. The Lang-dale Linen Industry changed its name to the Ruskin Linen Industry in his honour.

Two principal displays then await the visitor. Downstairs is a recon-structed Victorian street, complete with a Marks and Spencer's Penny Stall, and a chemist's with very fine fittings. Across the courtyard and through the craft shop is the Farm Barn, a gallery of agricultural implements, ploughs, harnesses, and carts. Notice how many of the plough blades, shafts and hand-les take the form of beautiful curving shapes. They look as if calculated by a mathematician with a taste for sculp-ture, but evolved over centuries as best fitted to help man and his animals haul weights and break up the ground, be-fore the coming of machines.

The wheelwright's shop

LANCASTER

Judges' Lodgings Museum

Church Street, Lancaster LA1 1YS
(0524) 32808
Open daily, afternoons, Easter to
October; also open mornings
Monday to Friday from July to
September. 🅶 ▣
♿ S: access very limited.
🚻 & 👫 phone to book in advance;
👫 contact the Education Officer
at the City Museum (0524) 64637.

Dundee Cabinet by Gillows of Lancaster, c.1872

Every county town council used to have
to make available lodgings for the cir-
cuit judges who travelled around to the
assize courts. The accommodation was
often not enviable: large chilly rooms,
lugubriously furnished, enlivened only
by yards of chintz, in gloomy Edwardian granges. In Lancaster, their
Lordships fared better. For very nearly
200 years, from 1776 to 1975, they had
the use of this fine town house, originally of 1639, which is now Judges'
Lodgings Museum. Traces of its fur-
nishing as judges' lodgings remain, but
it now houses in particular two unusual
collections. On the first floor, for the
most part, is the furniture of Gillows,
the Lancaster firm who set trends for
the whole country in the early 19th
century. Then at the top of the house is
a museum of childhood, with memorabilia of the nursery, schoolroom; and
play of all kinds.

The downstairs rooms display furnishings of a variety of periods. The
hall is distinguished by fine pieces of
oak furniture, and the parlour to the
right by panelling from about 1720. At
the back of the house, the servants' hall
and kitchen have been set out in the
manner of the early 19th century. The
wire mouse-trap is especially curious,
and worked on the principle of a lobs-
ter pot; the mouse might have been
caught, but was surely very much alive
to greet the first morning arrival in the
kitchen. In a display case in the corridor, with rare books, is a strange rarity.

Perambulator of about 1880

It is a large coin, a 17th century Thaler
of Augsburg, which has been delicately
machined so that it falls apart into two
halves, in order that the space inside
may be used for a thin, secret compartment. This was not wasted: inside were
no less than nine discs of the thinnest
mica, each painted with a little scene.
We see someone being apprehended,

and a scene of books being burnt. On
all but one of the discs the face of the
principal figure has been left un-
painted, and only appears when placed
over the one disc on which a face is
included on the figure. The discs must
hold the secrets of some proscribed
religious sect, or of the lodge of some
secret order, but for the moment secret
they remain. How were they to be
combined? What did they mean? Here
is an opportunity for a resourceful
sleuth with a little time to spare.

Upstairs are more furnished rooms,
beginning with the Senior Judge's bedroom. Surely no judicial bench in court
had a more portentous canopy than the
bed. All the same, the show is stolen in
these rooms by the Gillows furniture.
An especially rare piece, recently acquired, is a very fine Regency billiard
table by Gillows, complete with all
accessories – cue stands, billiard mar-
ker board, maces, cues, ivory balls –
the greatest assemblage in existence
from that period. Gillows began with a
bit of canny 18th century trading by
Robert Gillow. He was not one to miss
a trick. He imported mahogany from
the West Indies, turned it into furniture, then sent it back again, with other

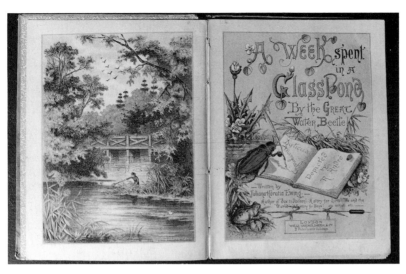

Cover of a children's picture book of the 1880s

merchandise packed into the drawers. His descendants and family kept the business going, with a London end to the operation, for a few generations, then sold out, leaving a concern that continued to flourish, until a slow decline in this century. In the 1840s Gillows supplied the Houses of Parliament, and in the 1930s helped with the luxury liner, the 'Queen Mary'.

A speciality was inlay in richly contrasting woods. The Dundee cabinet of 1870 is in baywood, with inlay of thuya and boxwood (colour plate 5), and there are examples of oak and of satinwood, with ivory inlay as well. Most of the furniture in the dining room, restored to its early-19th century appearance, is also by Gillows. There are plans in the near future to convert one of the rooms into a gallery of the history of the Gillow manufactory, and this will not only include furniture from the 18th century to the present day, but also a section that will display the construction of an individual piece from the preliminary drawings and templates to its completion. The centrepiece of this will be a bench complete with all the original tools, looking as if a cabinet maker was going to return to his work imminently.

Also on show is evidence of an extra service that Gillows offered their early 19th century clients. They would work out the entire decor of your drawing room, for example, drapes and furniture included, and prepare for you a pen and wash drawing, a kind of map of the room, with furniture in place. A speciality seems to have been, from the drawings here, the design of the elaborate swagging that hung over the windows, quite dwarfing the mere curtains. Although it seems unbelievable, they really did, in fact, hang up the yards and yards of gathered and ruffled stuff that we see in these drawings.

Upstairs, on the landing, a grand dolls' house ushers visitors into the museum of childhood, and we turn left into the schoolroom. You can sit at the little desks, and try out slates. On the walls, as well as warnings of the dangers of various diseases, are fine maps of the world. The landforms are so positively carpeted in minutely-printed names that it is hard to read any of them, but we can just make out such ancient territorial labels as 'Austro-Hungarian Monarchy'. There is a cupboard full of teaching aids. Not even cutting things out with scissors was allowed to be frivolous: here we find *Effective paper cutting*, by Anita and Henrietta Waite. The teaching was quite tough, even for young children. A page of dictation, in a new-looking script hand in an exercise book within one of the desks, records a real example of some long forgotten dictation lesson: 'The bane of the campaign was the disdain shown by inane commanders who would not dain [aha, that got them] to study the wily foe . . .' It was never too early to get to recognise pillars of public virtue, either. In the Edwardian Day Nursery, further down the passage, the toddlers' blackboard has a handle at the top for scrolling through pictures including portraits of such worthy men (no women in sight) as Gladstone and Lord Salisbury.

Still, they had it easy compared to some children, whose experiences are recalled in the Child's Play Room, along with the displays of toys. There is evidence of a girl brought up in the early 18th century, who wore from the ages of six to thirteen an iron collar round her neck, fastened to a board strapped to her back, to guarantee good posture, and who stood in this contraption for several hours a day during lessons. For poor children, much more recently, we learn that just playing in the streets was a crime, and the appearance of the policeman always a signal for flight.

This is to give a falsely gloomy account of the displays. There are plenty of happy reminiscences too, bringing to life the collections of dolls, prams and toys, and babycare of three centuries, which pack the rooms on this floor. The collection is being added to, under a scheme bringing together funding from the County Council and the Regional Arts Association, with toys made by contemporary craftspeople, which can be seen in the recent acquisitions room.

Wire mousetrap in the kitchen

Lancaster City Museum

Market Square, Lancaster LA1 1HT
(0524) 64637
Closed Sundays. **F**
♿ **S**: wheelchair access to ground
floor only.
🚻 & 🚻 must book, phone
Curator, 🚻 Education Officer.

Lancaster City Museum's most ardent
fan would not call it a glitzy institution.
It remains, as far as much of its display
goes, an example of museums as they
used to be. The collections are not so
much displayed, as set out for you to
use to make your own discoveries. It is
not, however, a place where the past
has been forgotten, but one in which it
is very much alive, if you pause to
discover it. The museum has a distinguished record in the encouragement of
enthusiasm for the history of Lancaster, and a tradition of publication of
knowledgeable pamphlets. The enthusiasm shows through in little details
within the displays, even if they sometimes look deceptively sleepy. The old
Town Hall is the home of the museum,
and the displays of archaeology, local
and military history upstairs are set in
ornate rooms, with representations of
the sources of Lancaster's prosperity
painted on the ceilings. The downstairs
space is used for the collections of fine
and applied art, or for imaginative temporary exhibitions. At the time of my
visit, it was given over to a popular
show on the history of motorbikes.

The staircase at that time presented
an unusual mixture of Roman material

18th century Bonheur-du-jour, *or lady's writing table, made by Gillows of Lancaster*

Hoard of 86 pennies wrapped in lead

and railway bygones, leading to a landing whose alcoves have been turned
into showcases. There is great sym-
pathy for the past in the choice of the
subjects to which each case is devoted.
The first makes a fascinating if grim
beginning with the processes of the
law. A scrap of printed ephemera records the outcome of the proceedings

at Lancaster Assizes at an unspecified
date, which must be within the first
years of the last century. Charles
Whalley, we read, was charged with
stealing at Manchester one mare, the
property of William Haslam. The ver-
dict was guilty, and, as for so many of
the defendants in this long list, the
entry ends with the laconic note: 'death

recorded'. Charles was eleven. Nearby is the very noose used for the public executions here between 1820 and 1830. There is a photograph of the chair, on wheels, used to take to execution Jane Scott, who killed her mother in 1828. To round it all off neatly, there is an invoice for the services of executioner Thomas Bennington at the execution of John Heyes. He seems to have sub-contracted with everyone else involved: there is £1.10s for the attendants in the prisoner's cell, five shillings for the constable, and eight pence for the cloth cap.

Nearby is a case of the least dramatic things imaginable, 'portabilia', just a collection of all the things that people might have carried around in pockets. An idea like this tells us more of daily life than acres of earnest labelling. There is a passport of 1872, still just a letter for brandishing around really, and two pocket pistols, handy if the foreigners did not get the hang of the passport. These examples had sensible fold-away triggers, not a feature you would want for high noon at the OK Corral, but prudent for more casual users who might otherwise blow away some part of their persons whilst merely rootling for change, or the door-key. There are tooth-picks and a cutter for quill pens, and a handy tiny tin box, containing a miniature pop-up candle and matches. And surely everyone would want, though hardly anyone would really need it, the miniature globe in a box with the constellations of the heavens pasted into the lid, 'a correct Globe, with Ye new constellations of Dr. Halley', which takes it back to the days of Isaac Newton.

Another alcove offers local Scotforth and Burton pottery, with a special line in the 'joke' puzzle jugs that poured a stream of beer over any drinker who didn't know that you have to drink out of a spout in the handle. These lively wares are usually decorated with characteristic trails of icing-like wet clay, or slip. Other alcoves offer local watch, clock and gun-making, walking sticks and umbrellas, bygones of the constabulary, and weights and measures.

These last represent centuries of the Office of Fair Trading in vestigial

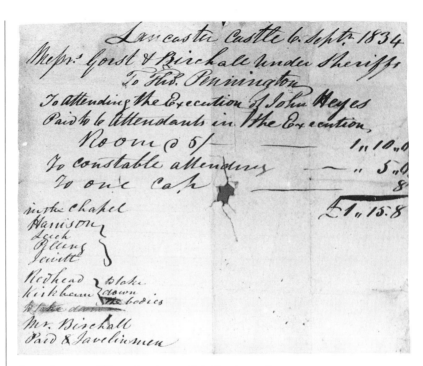

Invoice for services of Thomas Bennington at John Heyes's execution

form, and perhaps the authority of their mere availability did much to establish probity, and keep the peace in the market place. The handsome set of Corporation fluid and grain measures includes a corn gallon from as early as 1601. Nowadays standard measurements of length can be calibrated with reference to the interference of light waves, and subtleties of similarly suspect abstraction, but in the past it all came down to reassuring lengths of metal, agreed by everyone to be correct to a sliver of a whisker, and kept in velvet-lined boxes at places like Greenwich. A degree of precision appropriate to the market place was guaranteed by robust substitutes, and here they are, one foot, two feet and a yard in brass, guaranteed accurate at exactly 62 degrees farenheit, and handily kept, until transfer to the museum, on the wall of the police station.

The main historic material is kept in the room to the right, with the stocks. The history of the area is here from the

stone age to the present century. There are ceramics from prehistoric sites, including a fine collared urn, and some of the strange, utterly enigmatic gazing heads that were a Celtic speciality, adopted up here, too, by the Romans. In a case by itself are the remains of the Quernmore Burial, over a thousand years ago, discovered in 1973. The wood of the coffin is remarkably preserved, but of its contents nothing remains but the finely-woven shroud, and those bodily parts that grow for a while after death, as we see them here, large fragments of finger and toe-nails, and copious locks of luxuriant, dark, curly hair. Opposite, a little searching discovers a hoard of eighty-six silver pennies, buried in the middle ages in a sort of bag of soft lead. This might have been all the savings of someone modestly placed, or the fruits of a quite important transaction, concealed in those days long before safe banking was available against some rainy day. There are mementoes of the more gracious Lancaster of the 18th and

Prehistoric urn

19th centuries in the form of some items of furniture by the local firm of Gillows. The prosperous history of the town is summarised for this period by three models, comparing its extent in 1610 with the town of 1778 and 1821. Nearby, at this end of the room, is a huge wooden teapot, and a colossal wooden key, amongst other props that might come from Alice in Wonderland. They are shop signs, of the kind that used to hang in solid rows along the main shopping streets of every town, trying to do by sheer size the job done today by flourescent signs; the teapot was for a grocer's.

The other upstairs room displays the history of the 4th Regiment of Foot, the King's Own. They were prominent at Culloden, when Bonny Prince Charlie finally had to admit defeat, but they took one third of all the casualties of the occasion. A treasure here is the portrait, by the Lancashire portrait painter Arthur Devis, of the man who led them on that occasion and lost a hand in the process, Sir Robert Rich (ill. on cover). It is typical of Devis's lucid, glowing little portraits. Most vivid evidence of the local regiments' later history is in the hinged frames of photographs through which one may browse, taking them through the two World Wars of this century.

Lancaster Maritime Museum

Saint George's Quay, Lancaster LA1 1RB   (0524) 64637
Closed mornings November to March. 🔊 🖼
♿ W: wheelchair access to all but mezzanine floor.
🚻 & 👥 must book, 🚻 phone Curator, 👥 Education Officer.

Lancaster's new Maritime Museum is installed on the old quay, in a restored custom house of 1764, designed by Richard Gillow of the famous Lancaster furniture family, and an adjoining warehouse. It offers an enormous amount of information about the local area and its maritime associations, on well-prepared panels of text and images, with plenty of three-dimensional reconstructions, besides historic objects and audio-visual aids. There is even a tank full of live specimens, to show the marine life of the area. Outside there are real boats.

A visit can begin in the grand, central long room of the old custom house, into which captains would come with their papers. Visitors are greeted by a colourful figurehead (ill. on cover), and there are ship models, a fine painting of 'Lancaster from Cable Street' by Julius Caesar Ibbetson, and for children, a computer quiz, with a choice of three different games. In rooms to the left are a reconstruction of the office of the port's controller, and displays about the nature of local trade. The slavery that regrettably contributed so much to England's prosperity in the

Model of 'Thetis', an armed merchant ship

Women picking shrimps, c.1926

later 18th century was conspicuous here, as in other west coast ports. On the other side of the hall is a model of the whole Morecambe Bay area, with push-buttons to illuminate centres of development at different periods.

Morecambe Bay and Heysham are described in more detail at the top of the warehouse, reached from the custom house via an outside passage and lift. There are six modern drawings, cleverly presenting the bay from the same spot at six different dates, from 1000 BC to 1980 AD, along with information and mementoes of costume, entertainment and travel connected with the seaside in recent times. Wildlife, animal and vegetable, is shown as well. In the next room, by contrast, modern brightly-coloured metal structures provide a setting for a high-tech display about the recovery and processing of undersea gas, which comes ashore at Heysham. A large panel lights up to present an animated account of the complex processes by which the gas, initially mixed with water vapour and undesirable contaminants, is conducted and prepared for consumption.

The next room provides a staircase for access to a temporary exhibition area, and otherwise contains a reconstruction of a warehouse scene, with dockers handling barrels. The barrel was a brilliant as well as beautiful invention, waterproof, immensely resistant to stress from inside or outside, and manoeuvreable by muscle power. Each size of barrel was used for goods of a particular kind, so that a knowledgeable eye could readily judge a

Reconstruction of a warehouse scene, with dockers

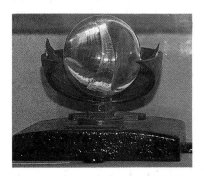

Sunshine recorder

cargo, and its weight. The next room contains another life-size reconstruction, this time of one of the four packet-boats that, just before the coming of the railways, provided the fastest transport from Lancaster to Preston, or Kendal, doing the thirty miles in about three hours. At two shillings (10p) one way – three shillings if you wanted a quilted seat in the first class bit – it was not so cheap when a labourer's family were doing well if they had fifty pounds a year, but the quiet trip in the airy cabin must have been a delight. For the horses pulling the boats it was tougher, as recounted in a recorded commentary with an account of this mode of travel, which visitors can listen to inside the cabin. There is a sound commentary in the next display, about the coach service across Morecambe Sands. Finally on this floor, there is a room that you can share with the figure of a sailor, who seems to be asleep, to watch two audio-visual presentations, a

nine-minute 'Story of the Port of Lancaster', and a seven-minute history of Morecambe Bay, from the Romans, who called it the Great Bay, to the area of today, as seen from a satellite.

A long staircase leads down to the shop, and in the basement of the custom house to displays about the fishing economy, with a reconstruction of the hearth of a fisherman's cottage in about 1925. There are fishing nets, and a spectacular corner array of the beautifully-turned wooden tools that the boat-builders used. Just before another staircase, leading us upwards, we can find out about cockling, and see the cocklers jumbo and cram. The former is a wooden board, flat on one side, handy handles on the other, for pounding the sand to bring the cockles to the surface in winter. The cram is a short stick with little curved prongs on the end, for winkling them out. The staircase brings us back into the central long room of the custom house.

LEYLAND

The British Commercial Vehicle Museum

King Street, Leyland, Preston, Lancashire PR5 1LE
(0772) 451011
Closed October to March inclusive, except for weekends in October and November; closed Mondays April to September.
🅿 ♿ W
♿ & ♿ phone to give notice of visits and to request pre-visit 'school-pack'; can sometimes be booked when museum is otherwise closed.

General view of the British Commercial Vehicle Museum

Have you ever wondered, whilst casting an eye over a collection of used cars in a sale-room, whether the squeaky clean vehicle you decide to buy is really as good as new, or whether it has actually taken a frightful bending? Some of the gleaming vehicles in this museum really have been through the kind of experiences you have nightmares about after you have made your purchase: bodywork in a hedge for forty-seven years, chassis in a yard nearby, engine found at the bottom of a lake. Thousands of hours of dedicated work by enthusiasts have gone into some of the exhibits here, so that rescued vehicles, as well as cherished and pampered ones sparkle. It is a spectacle in the large hangar-like display space. The selection runs from horse-drawn carts to British Leyland's Technology Demonstrator, with computer screens in the cab and video rear-view camera, enough to give anyone a bit of an itch to be a 21st century truck driver.

Heavy work until the end of the 1920s required steam vehicles. James Watt, who invented the kind of steam engine that powered all those cotton mills you may have been visiting in the area, was rightly appalled at speculation that the idea might be applied to

road vehicles. He even put into the lease of his house a prohibition on approach within fifty feet of it by any steam carriage. They were duly developed all the same. The ones that made the grade were not like locomotives, but were fuelled by engines running on petroleum-type fuel. Traction engines, like big steam tractors, are familiar stars of country shows, but the steam vans and lorries here are less familiar. The Thornycroft steam van for 1-ton loads of 1896 makes no real secret of its odd parentage. It was built by ship-builders, powered by an engine for a steam-boat, and looks like a cart with a funnel on it. Dozens of vehicles of the type were made over the next twenty years. Tate and Lyle's Foden 6 tonner of 1922 is a grand example, no

1921 Model T Ford van

longer looking like a steam-powered cart, but like a locomotive on the roads. It was driven from the right of the cab, steered from the left, and weighed more than it could carry. It is also rather beautiful, with an ogee-form tapering nose ending in a funnel at the front. These vehicles are the dinosaurs of road haulage. There is in addition a rare evolutionary 'missing link' here, unsuccessful, but on the right track – a Beardmore Cobra of 1931, trying to turn into an articulated lorry. In 1984 it toured the country as Marks and Spencer's centenary truck.

There are lighter vans as well. You would have been in for a surprise if you had tried to drive off in a Ford T van assuming that you knew your way around the three pedals. The left hand pedal selected low gear when pushed to the floor, neutral half way up and top fully released; the middle pedal, instead of being a brake, put you into reverse; the right hand one was a brake, acting on the transmission. A hand lever gave drive when forward, neutral in the middle, and acted as a brake on the rear wheels when pulled back. If you really thought you had enough arms and legs to handle all that and steer at the same time, all you needed was one extra hand, for the accelerator lever on the steering column. There is plenty of properly technical information about many of the vehicles, so enthusiasts can pore over the minutiae. You do not need to be an engineer, however, to fail to be fooled by the Ford Transit Supervan 2. This is not a goods vehicle at all. Look through the rear windows to see the goods compartment almost completely filled with the gigantic engine, eight huge cylinders giving 3955 cc and a top speed of 186 mph. The dinky blue seat belts are charmingly embroidered.

Horse bus of 1896

The fire engines are fun, and it is reassuring to see that they had crank handles, which the crew could leap off and resort to if necessary. (How daft they must all feel today, sitting there raring to go in their shiny helmets when the engine won't start.) Merryweather had this market taped, it seems, with hand-drawn, horse-drawn, and even steam-powered specimens in the 19th century. By 1938 they turned out a very dashing line in turntable pumps. The borough of Barking bought one, which saw them through the blitz and beyond, until its well-earned retirement here. It is an open-top model, with comfy padded seats, and if it was not your turn to drive, you might at least be allowed to turn the handle to ring the big brass bell. The buses are good too. Once again, there is a horse-drawn one to set the scene, a beautiful and sedate thing from Edinburgh. There are familiar double-deckers, which did loyal local service in the 1920s and '30s, displayed against a

background of their unrolled destination banners, and you can climb into a single decker, which did 1,597,843 miles around Lisbon between 1948 and 1985.

Then there are the exotica. Peer through the windows of a showman's living wagon of 1912 (colour plate 6). It must have been a bit cramped after a while, but the accommodation was nothing if not compact. The bedroom has painted wooden panelling, and a little privacy provided by decorative frosted glass; the cosy living room even has a real range-type stove. Franz de Cap's Belgian automatic dance organ, a profusion of mirrors and lights, with accordion, organ, cymbals and drum, still tours local venues. In the opposite corner of the hangar, climb aboard British Leyland's special Papal transport, the famous Pope-mobile of the 1982 UK visit. It's really just a customised 24.15 ton Constructor Three-axle Tipper Chassis. Up on the VIP passenger deck, though, is a bit of special fitting, a kind of shooting-stick affair anchored into the floor, with handles in front for balance, and a leather bottom rest. If by this stage in the visit a little rest is in order, you can park yours where he parked his.

Dotted around the displays are interesting and surprising oddments and

1896 Thornycroft steam van

photographs, bringing alive the motoring world of decades ago. A gallon of petrol cost one shilling and tuppence – about 6p – from the Esso petrol pump here, and there is a photograph nearby of a similar pump outside a thatched gas station. Perhaps the most engaging document records a bit of recklessness in Liverpool Road, Salford, on 6th February 1914. It duly led to a summons for 3-toner driver Thomas Knox, who did unlawfully, it was alleged, proceed 'on the highway there situate at a speed exceeding 5 miles per hour, to wit at a speed of 7 miles 251 yards per hour ... contrary to a certain regulation.'

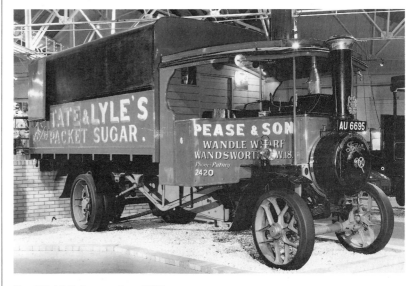

Tate & Lyle's Foden steam lorry, 1922

LIVERPOOL

Large Objects Collection

Princes Dock, Liverpool, Merseyside
L3 0AA   (051) 207 0001
Closed November to Easter. ▣
◼   ♿ W
♿ & ♿ must book in advance; may
be bookable during months of
closure; phone ext. 263.

Do you hate packaging? If you are a
practical person, perhaps a bit technically minded, who hates having to
find a way into a glossy confection of
cardboard and acetate just to get at
half-a-dozen nails, then the Large Object Collection in Liverpool is your
museum. It presents its contents totally
unpackaged. Gone are the acres of
designer captioning, the carpets, the
expensive light fittings, and the refusal
to put on display anything that has not
first been cosmetically restored. There
are no showcases, because very few of
the exhibits would fit in them. The
museum consists of two huge sheds
full of everything from farm carts to a
Blue Streak rocket, crammed together
and packed to the roof, with racks of
mysterious parts glimpsed in the background. One section, even, is just called 'Bits and pieces'. The museum is
also the home of Technology Testbed,
one of the first 'hands-on' displays, of
the kind developed in the United
States, now slowly coming to Europe.
Liverpool's version is tailored to complement the large objects in the collection, and consists of about eighty
experiments, which you try out for
yourself, to find out the often surprising scientific principles behind the
museum's objects.

    You spent a lot of money on the Blue
Streak rocket, if you paid tax through
the 1960s, and now you can see that at
least there was certainly a lot of it. The
section here is as big as a whale, and
the strange turbo pumps from its works
alongside look a bit like what you might
imagine a whale's intestines to be, at
least in a nightmare; which, of course,
is where this rocket belonged, since its

A printing demonstration in progress

Telescopes among the Large Objects

sole original purpose was to dump a
nuclear warhead on someone. The objects opposite also look a bit like rockets, of a rather cranky kind, the type of
thing the Victorians would have built
for the job. They are indeed from the

last century, but these are peaceful
chunks of metal, a collection of the
giant telescopes that wealthy amateurs
had made for themselves. The earliest
is Captain James Huddart's, of 1797.
Sir John Herschel managed to use it
for pioneering observations of double
star systems twenty years later; but
most of these huge instruments, all
state-of-the-art for their day, were piti-
fully wasted in the English climate.
There are small reflecting telescopes
alongside for visitors to look through.
The collections round about offer
dozens of strange contrasts of objects,
with vintage fish-and-chip shop fittings
in one place, and what look like church
furnishings glimpsed in another. A
favourite for me was the riot shield on
wheels of 1911, called 'The Gladstone', presumably in an effort by its
makers to endow it with the righteous
authority inseparable from that statesman's name.

    The collection is especially strong in
vehicles of every kind. There is a row
of bicycles, from those similar to the
penny farthing to the article familiar to

us today, and a whole depot of vintage buses and trams. The museum makes a small concession to display here, forgiveable even if it is the latest in fashion for transport museum decor. A line of those alphabetical lists of stops on rolls of fabric, which the bus crews unwound to display the destinations fore and aft, are unrolled and used as covering for a few hundred square feet of wall. Groups of names, such as Dingle, Edge Lane, Fazakerly, Garston and Gillmoss, read like free-verse poems, thanks to the suggestive qualities that place names always have for strangers. The earliest of the public transport vehicles in this section are horse-drawn trams, Liverpool's with a Sunlight Soap advert gleaming from the riser of every stair, Birkenhead's with delicate wrought iron-work around its open top. The Leyland Lioness of 1927, set apart as is proper, only became a bus in 1930 after a career carrying more distinguished loads: it was George V's baggage van.

Experimenting at Technology Testbed

You could cope with a small disaster with the emergency vehicles that are here, with steam rollers and access towers galore for the cleaning up afterwards. If you are not into engineering, concentrate on the early horse-drawn coaches. A gorgeous yellow one made in the 1860s for four-in-hand riding did a stint in the '90s as a stage-coach, even if no further west than on the Shrewsbury to Chester run. Liverpool

Corporation's natty black two-seater Brougham of 1890 offers something especially artistic. The linkage between suspension and steering is a feast for the connoisseur of curves, offering overlapping circles, S shapes and ogees, as well as the usual gently curving springs, all picked out in red trim on the black.

If your interest in curves is scientific too, there is a special display near the telescopes. At the back of a dark tent, vintage computer gear winks and hums, and in the middle, what looks like a huge photographic enlarger projects a pattern onto a table. Not so long ago scientists pored over these patterns twenty-four hours a day. They are photographs of streaks, which revealed the paths of sub-atomic particles in something like the way that vapour trails betray high-flying planes, in a special tank at the CERN research facility in Switzerland. Nowadays the paths are recorded by computer as they are made, but until a few years ago collections of equipment, like this one devised by Liverpool University, were needed to computerise the hundreds of thousands of photographs. One of the pictures is displayed where we may study it. The tell-tale trails are curved because the particles that made them were charged ones, sensitive to a magnetic field in the tank. The tighter the curve, the weaker the energy of the particle and the less it could resist the pull of the magnetic field. Long, gentle parallel curves dominate the scene, anti-protons streaking through undisturbed at a high proportion of the speed of light. The curves are beaded with tiny spirals – the paths of weak particles, thrown into a spin by the passing anti-protons. One anti-proton did not get through so easily. It firmly collided with some particle in the tank, giving rise to a cascade of later collisions and annihilations, traced for us through a succession of symmetrical curves, which end in a large graceful spiral as an energetic positron succumbs to the field.

The Test-bed experiments, scattered through both sheds, and outside as well, give you a tangible experience of the forces of nature. You can feel

how arrangements of pulleys make lighter work of lifting, explore the supporting qualities of bridges of different kinds, and solve a problem you've never worried about, how a giraffe manages to get liquid up that long neck when it drinks. Before you visit all those industrial heritage textile museums, try out for yourself the little loom here, to really understand how they worked. Do not wear your Sunday best. Outside are the water experiments, four of them operated by flushing an amazing 'Heath-Robinson' arrangement of tanks on a pole, to set in motion a bucket spun like a liquid Catherine-wheel, or make two tall tanks go into competition to see which can squirt water into the other. If you are brave, you can ride on a water-jet-propelled rocket; and if you are brave, but do not want to get wet, just ride a bicycle on a trapeze wire. Do not expect everything to be working. These experiments take a tremendous pounding, and are constantly being improved; no display of their kind anywhere manages to have everything going at once. With eighty-odd things to chose from, everyone can still expect to find something surprising and fascinating.

1920s fish & chip dispenser

Around the museum are notes from children, written after visits. One says, 'I like the rokets the best and the roket bike was gud to and the lenses were gud to and i thort the [telephones] was gud to . . .' That's a testimonial worth taking seriously.

Liverpool Museum

William Brown Street, Liverpool,
Merseyside L3 8EN
(051) 207 0001
Open daily. V for Planetarium performances. W
& phone Education Officer (ext. 211) to book and for information about extensive services.

The collections of Liverpool Museum are so varied that it is easier to describe what they leave out than to list what they include: of the typical collections found in traditional museums, painting is up the road at the **Walker Art Gallery**, and maritime history has its own museum, the **Merseyside Maritime Museum**, in the Albert Dock; but otherwise it is just about all here. All, that is, that can be shown in the space available, for Liverpool has collections in store second to none outside London. The quality of what is on show is therefore very high. The displays are all up-to-date. The building was damaged by bombing in World War Two, and reopened only in the late 1960s. Since then, it has enjoyed a lively and experimental approach to display, which has resulted in a number of quiet innovations, especially recently, which other museums are sure to follow.

A visit might begin downstairs in the aquarium, with exquisite vividly striped and spotted tropical fish exploring huge sheets of Australian coral reef, and fish from our own chillier waters exploring a wreck. Next door is a transport gallery, with everything from an elegant two-seater chariot of the middle of the last century to a locomotive. Climbing to the ground floor we find an introduction to the collections, and mementoes of the King's Liverpool Regiment. This gallery covers the history of one of the oldest regiments of the regular British Army, formed as Earl Ferrer's 8th Foot in 1685, and includes sections on all the major campaigns in which the King's Regiment took part. The museum has also developed a gallery for major temporary

The Natural History Centre at Liverpool Museum

exhibitions on this floor. Forthcoming exhibitions will include Bulgarian Traditional Art, the Archaeology of Jordan, and Carthage.

To the left of the main entrance are the new ceramic galleries. The main room displays the most extraordinary pieces in the collection, in just a few cabinets. Each cabinet is tall, so that a great deal can be shown without overcrowding, and shows a group of works that offer interesting comparisons. Medieval potters and their 17th century successors, who decorated their wares with liquid trails of clay, or 'slip', like icing on a cake, had to have decorative schemes clear in their minds, as the slip dried fast; their pieces can be seen together here. Later wares offer some different lessons. A gleaming white parian-ware group caught my eye, of 'Britomart unveiling Amoret' (1851): it is like a text-book example of what feminist art historians advise us to look out for. He is resplendent and active in armour, she naked, passive and defenceless – only there at all, really, as a prop to show off male nobility. The fact that in this piece he, for some reason, looks disgusted and she looks drugged, cannot prevent it from illuminating some of the meanings that works of art can have. There is tons more of this kind of thing in the **Walker Art Gallery**. Did the Victorians go in for it because the women in their society were completely dominated by the male? Or was it a fantasy escape from growing realisation that their womenfolk, riding bicycles, wearing plus-fours and cropping their hair by the end of the century, meant it when they said they wanted the vote? For more technical information about the ceramics on show in the room, and the processes of making them, visitors can refer to a computerised information system installed in the gallery. A further gallery beyond displays the whole reserve collection as an archive, case after case, shelf after shelf – a treat for the enthusiast, and a spectacle for anyone.

The first floor of the museum is devoted to human artefacts from all over the world, including an exceptional display of Greek and Roman statuary. It is unusual for an English regional museum to have such items at all, and they are displayed in a circular setting, with lighting that dims and brightens around the circle as time passes, giving an effect of changing sunlight. It is also stimulating to be presented with these ancient pieces not only as the culmination of a succession

Skeleton of the dinosaur, Allosaurus

Benin sculpture, early 16th century

of displays showing more archaic Mediterranean material, but also in the context of objects exhibited from many other cultures. What was it about Greece and the islands nearby that provided the impetus to make such realistic statues for the first time? You can look for clues as you trace your steps back in time past the earlier wares of the region. Do you detect

some new kind of rational approach to life in the beautifully simple interlocking circles on some earlier Cypriot pots? And have we in the process lost some of the intensity of a more intuitive approach to life? Ceremonial masks and figures from the Pacific are accompanied by challenging information; terrifying though they may seem to us, we cannot imagine the depth of terror they inspired in the participants of the rituals for which they were made. There are things, too, from other centralised cultures, including very fine Benin bronzes from 16th century Nigeria, extraordinary virtuoso feats of metal casting, yielding figure sculptures as fine as any.

The second floor has natural history, explaining evolution and showing many species in different habitats of today, from the Arctic to the tropics. The evolution display is frankly intended to teach, but tells its story in different ways for different audiences, with a computer quiz to finish. The specimens in their habitats are a less demanding feast for the eyes. On no account miss the sea mouse, Britain's bulkiest and most horrid worm, which lives in the sand. Museums have found it difficult to provide displays based on

Early 13th century reliquary casket

their botanical collections. Herbarium specimens rarely form exciting exhibits, but at Liverpool the problem has been overcome by enclosing part of the gallery to provide a separate environment for growing living plants.

If you pick the right day, you may be able to get into the museum's new

Natural History Centre, where there are dozens of drawers that you can open to see more specimens, and things to touch and do. Discover that the hippo has a wobbly tooth in his huge skull, or try to put a badger skeleton together, like a jig-saw, using the template provided. There are more real specimens, like the wing of a dragonfly, to examine through microscopes, or to show to a television camera for a magnified view on a screen. For anyone with a more specialist interest, a second room contains cabinets with drawer after drawer of specimens to study. Watch other museums struggle to catch up with this idea. During 1989, it is hoped to open the Centre every afternoon, Tuesday to Sunday inclusive.

The top floor is for time and space (and a cup of coffee). The timekeeping displays are outside the cafeteria, rocketry around the corner. Plans are underway to redisplay the Space Gallery during 1990. The present displays offer, among other things, an instructive comparison between the nicely-rounded, unused nose-cone of a Black Knight rocket, and a similar nose-cone after impact with the ground, delicately corrugated. Outside the Planetarium entrance is a view of Merseyside from space, and beside it a special treat, live television pictures from Meteosat, a satellite that hangs forever above the equator over Africa, looking north, to provide a weather image of the European quadrant of the globe, from North Africa to the North Pole. First it slowly builds up, line by line, a view of the whole scene, then of one sixth of it at a time, taking twenty minutes to complete a cycle. England is quite foreshortened from this perspective, but there is no difficulty in making it out, and seeing an interesting phenomenon: even if the whole country is otherwise cloudless, you will almost always see a little ruffle of cloud, a mere fluff on this scale, bunched up against the Pennines where the warm air stream from the Atlantic is carried upwards into cooler, overlying layers. And that is why there is no place like the North West for exploring museums.

Merseyside Maritime Museum

Albert Dock, Liverpool, Merseyside L3 4AA   (051) 207 0001
Parts of the site are closed November to April. Because of the nature of the site, children under 16 must be accompanied. 🔊 ▣
🅿 (for Albert Dock)
♿ : wheelchair access good to most parts of site.
🚾 & 🚻 phone Education Service to book and for information on facilities and programmes. ☺

Merseyside Maritime Museum is huge, with attractions spread over six dockside locations. The main historical displays are in the Albert Warehouse. Nearby is the Piermaster's house, with offices, suitably furnished, and with demonstrations of cooperage (barrel-making) to the rear. There are more displays in the Pilotage Bulding, and you can see workshops in the Boat Hall, besides, for most of the year, visiting the quays, and exploring the

pilot vessel, 'Edmund Gardner'. The sites are all around the series of pools making up the docks, and visitors make their way (with a sharp eye on small children) along a maze of quays and across giant tidal gates. The site itself is not upstaged by any museum, anywhere. The Albert Dock, in particular, is a masterpiece of 1840s architecture, and beyond it is the Mersey Estuary. Reflections glitter off every surface when the sun shines, and the whole site is hauntingly atmospheric when it doesn't.

Inside the Albert Warehouse we can lift handsets at a model of the docks, to learn how it all worked. Ships entered and left the complex at high tide, via the main river entrance gates, which were otherwise closed – as they still are – to stop the water level in the docks dropping with the tide. Albert was the unloading dock, and from there ships passed through into Salthouse Dock behind for loading, then round to Canning Dock and Half-Tide basin to await high tide. King John got the thing going in a rudimentary way, as we discover one floor up in 'The Evolution of the Port', for an attack on Ireland.

Exterior view of the Merseyside Maritime Museum

Displays chronicle the rise of the port. Slaving was a tragic part of it, with 303,737 slaves shipped from Liverpool between 1783 and 1793 alone. There are details and a model showing the frightful conditions in which they made the crossing. The prosperity of the later port depended on the industrial hinterland, its network of canals, and above all on the Lancashire cotton industry.

Another floor up is 'Builders of the Great Ships', with a multi-screen video presentation from the Cammell Laird shipyards, and displays of many other builders. This is the place for engine enthusiasts, with small masterpieces in modelling of side lever, oscillating cylinder and triple expansion engines. There is a fine example of the real thing too, a compound engine for the paddle-driven steam yacht, 'Firefly II' of 1900. This is one for artists as well as engineers, a sculptural assembly of giant pistons and tiny pipes in every metal finish, matt, shiny silver and brass, with black, white and blue paintwork. The smooth engineering of the engine contrasts with the spidery paddles, still attached, rough with old rust under black paint. It has 9 and 18 inch cylinders, with a 20 inch stroke delivering 12 nominal horsepower at 140 psi, and they made it up the river, in Runcorn.

Exhibitions are also shown on this floor – 'Art and the Sea' when I visited, with figureheads as well as pictures displayed. The oil paintings by Chinese artists who flourished in the ports around the Pacific and Indian Oceans were unusual, more patterned than work by their European contemporaries. The English 19th century views of Liverpool and Whitehaven were particularly good, the former showing a cluster of windmills not far from the Dock, to the north of the city. One treasure, properly used downstairs in 'Builders of the Great Ships', though it could be shown here as well, is the cased model of the two-masted schooner, 'Sarah', made by an unknown sailor in 1838. Surrealist artists only got around to making magic boxes like this a century later. Sarah herself is fine, but the scene is a poetic fantasy of

A cooper demonstrating his craft, barrel-making

the sea-shore, with a fort and buglers, sea-shells, dogs, children and a lighthouse. The maker used whatever toy figures and cut-outs came to hand, so that the scale changes. A row of ships under full sail scuds across the bottom in the very foreground of the scene.

Upstairs again is 'Safe Passage', about safety in the Port. A video shows how it feels to be in charge, using the radar scanners, but it was not always so controlled. Disasters are related in the displays, and to tidy up afterwards there is a Siebe-Gorman diving suit. The diver stayed down with the aid of leaden boots, and big lead weights tied around him, like the heart-shaped one on the chest of this suit. Air was pumped down by hand with the wooden device shown alongside. Amongst the other equipment, the Norwegian Pattern Hand-cranked Rotary Fog-horn looks fun. It is like an early movie camera with the handle on the side, and a speaker tube at the front where the lens would be. It was not exactly automatic. 'The regulation blasts can be separated', the instructions explain, 'and the length of each

Reconstruction of emigrants on ship

blast determined, by stopping the turning of the handle.' Those Norwegians would never have thought that one out without the instructions!

'Emigrants to a New World' is the most spectacular display, with a spooky alley-way reconstruction at its heart, leading to accommodation like that in which 19th century steerage passengers would have made the crossing. Sounds, smells and hunched figures conjure up something of the congestion amongst the rows of stacked double bunks. Other displays explain why people had no choice but to go, and relate, with real life examples, what they found on the other side of the Atlantic. There are especially good details of the crossing. We can lift a 'phone to hear William Greenhalgh's diary of a voyage to Australia in 1853, when complaints about the dish-water-like soup were met with threats of leg-irons. Better things were promised in the leaflets of Gracey Beasley and Co.'s packet boats: 1 lb of beef for each passenger, which sounds pretty good till you read that this is only on some days, and then there was no flour, rice, raisins, peas, suet or vinegar. It was better with Cunard in the 1920s. Advertising film shows the lap of luxury, with steward service, it is stressed, even in the third-class dining room. If your own ancestors may have gone through some of this, the display includes a computerised introduction to the Emigration Bureau, with hints on how to trace the ancestors. More displays are under preparation in this building, including a ship model gallery and the history of the port from 1857 to 1989.

In the Piermaster's house across the entrance to Albert Dock is a Victorian interior, complete with a costumed interpreter on some days, hissing gas lamps, and a pier-master, presumably, in bed upstairs. Outside, at the back, you can find out how barrels are made from an expert. Across the entrance to the river, the Pilotage House shows temporary displays. At the time of writing, these are of the collections formed by the Wynn Family at Fort Belan, built in 1775 to guard the Menai Strait. Amongst the odd items is a gunning punt, of 1907. There is a chest of gunshot, wadding and charge in the punt (but whatever was the 'Colgate's Demulgent Shaving Tablet' used for?). The gun is just an eight-foot-long tube, two inches in diameter. It looks like overkill for ducks, and it was. Its record was 140 with one shot. Beyond the Pilotage building is the Boat Hall, the quaysides, and the Pilot Cutter 'Edmund Gardner'. Once on board, you can explore everything from the accommodation to the engine room.

Merseyside Museum of Labour History

Islington, Liverpool, Merseyside
L3 8EE   (051) 207 0001
Open daily. ⛶ ♿
♿ & ♿ phone Education Officer to book and for information on special services and facilities.

All too often, the view of the past we gain from museums is predominantly that of the privileged. Theirs are the tombs, clothing, furnishings and documents that tend to have survived, and when evidence of the lives of ordinary working people appears at all, it often suggests that the bulk of the population merely played a supporting role as anonymous servants, workers and soldiers, in the important drama of the life of the well-to-do. The Merseyside Museum of Labour History was founded to present life on Merseyside from the point of view of the majority of people who lived there in the past, for the majority of people who live there now. It offers a sharp and unmissable addition to the august avenue of museums and galleries on central Liverpool's William Brown Street.

For a start, it is wonderfully installed in the old County Sessions House. It is appropriate, since even those who do not see the whole legal system as a mechanism for the oppression of the

Women working in a tobacco factory, early 20th century

The Officers of the Liverpool Trades Council, c.1936

majority would not deny that legal decisions have occasionally been tinged with class prejudice. For those unfamiliar with the courts, it is a revelation. The whole building, designed by the Borough Surveyor's department and built in 1884, appears to have been contrived so as to maximise the dramatic and theatrical aspects of the business (although the aim, in fact, was to keep the various users separate). As a panel of information on the main landing explains, there are four entrances, mean and humble ones at the back for prisoners, their families and the public, a respectable one at the side for lawyers and witnesses, and a splendid one in front, for their honours and worships and learned counsel. A spaghetti junction of staircases – closed with a grill for the prisoners, decently tiled for the folk from the side door, magnificently panelled for the front door classes – ensured that everyone could get in and out without embarrassing or insecure encounters with one another taking place. Bright panelled rooms with splendid plaster ceilings were provided for the out-of-court moments of judges, magistrates and senior staff. At the heart of the building is the main courtroom, huge, irredeemably gloomy, neatly divided into boxed enclosures for judges, witnesses, defendants, jury, county bigwigs, and so forth, each furnished with seats of appropriate status. In here you can imagine yourself in whichever roles you feel comfortable, or uncomfortable.

The courtroom now makes a convenient display area for the museum's collection of trade association and union banners, which need the space, and can be shown continuously without fading in its subdued lighting. Nearby the bright Magistrates' Meeting Room houses displays of political history, including the police strike in Liverpool in 1919, when tanks were brought in. Across the Landing, the Library now houses a reconstruction of a simple Edwardian schoolroom, with old desks, and even a schoolmaster.

Downstairs, where a visit commences, you first enter a space for temporary exhibitions. From there, you

Tired Mothers' Holiday Fund

WE are all planning OUR HOLIDAYS except the WORKING MOTHER

SHE WANTS YOUR HELP.

The Home where Holidays are unknown.

A Corner in the Garden— Tired Mothers Haven.

"I did not know there were so many trees in the World."

"It was like Heaven—nothing to do but rest me and baby."

CHEQUES, POSTAL ORDERS, STAMPS, TO
MARGARET BEAVAN,
TIRED MOTHERS' HOLIDAYS,
Office : 9, Copperas Hill, LIVERPOOL.
﹖e THREE SHILLINGS for ONE DAY if you can't give a Guinea.

BECAUSE—
She cooks, and washes, and scrubs, and sews the year through WITHOUT ANY REST.

BECAUSE—
There is always a STRUGGLE TO MAKE ENDS MEET.

BECAUSE—
The WELL-BEING of the children DEPENDS on her. She has NEVER in her LIFE HAD A HOLIDAY.

Can you spare One Guinea to give her one week's rest?

DO YOU MEAN THAT I AM TO HAVE A HOLIDAY?

Fundraising poster for Tired Mothers' Holiday Fund

can squeeze your way to the left down a paved alleyway lined with blown-up photographs of alleys and courts in Victorian Liverpool, to discover displays suggesting how people sometimes succeeded, sometimes failed, to live with decency in terrible conditions. A model, made in the 1920s to explain

Photograph of a domestic servant

Walker Art Gallery

William Brown Street, Liverpool
L3 8EL   (051) 207 0001
Open daily. Ⓥ ▣
♿ : access by rear entrance and
goods lift at present (although
better access is planned); make
arrangements in advance with
Head Warder or his Assistant.
🚻 & 🚹 contact Education Service
for information. ◎

If you like art galleries, you will like the
Walker. It is a place where the policy
has been to let pictures and sculptures
speak for themselves, and the collections are very fine. In a roll call of great
names, one might include Simone
Martini, Michelangelo, Rembrandt,
Poussin, Gainsborough, Turner and
Degas. There are some particularly
famous and familiar English pictures,
such as Hogarth's painting of the actor
Garrick as Richard III, recoiling from a
nightmare, Millais's Pre-Raphaelite
'Isabella', and Albert Moore's masterpiece, 'A Summer Night'. Amongst
pictures that are well known, though by
lesser artists, one might include
Yeames's 'And when did you last see

your father?', showing the small son of
a Royalist being interrogated by Parlia-
mentarians in the English Civil War,
and a picture that absolutely obsessed
D.H. Lawrence, of a girl being grap-
pled by a hairy-looking rural chap, 'An
Idyll', by Maurice Greiffenhagen.
There are also good English 20th century works, and important exhibitions,
especially the John Moores shows of
contemporary art. The gallery has recently begun to produce a series of
video-tapes, with distinguished contemporary artists discussing their
works in the collection.

One way for a non-specialist to
approach such a general but rich collection is to choose a theme and wander around with that theme in mind.
Something to look for in pictures of
any period are patterns – not just completely regular patterns, like wallpaper
repeats, but areas of the surface where
similar shapes reoccur in a disorga-
nised way, as in a marbling pattern.
Since pictures are flat things, patterned
patches are unavoidable if the picture
represents patterned subjects. Many
artists also took advantage of the way
that a less obviously patterned subject,
like plain drapery, which tends to seem
disordered in the three-dimensional

the conditions, lets us look down on a
maze of alleys carved like narrow
grooves in a block of dwellings. On the
far side of the exhibition area a passage
leads to a reconstruction of yet more
grim living conditions, vividly described in a report of 1842, in which
poor families lived in cellars that were
little more than caves.

There are also displays of what life
was like for those who were able to find
work. All kinds of callings are represented, even clerical work, with one of
the earliest dictaphones, nearly a century old, which enabled dictation to be
recorded on a wax cylinder. Most of
the mementoes are of manual labour.
Especially vivid are the simple-looking
hooks of the dockers. As a recollection
accompanying them explains, it was
vital to get the right one: 'The main
thing as a docker was the hook. You
had to have a good hook, which would
fit your hand, and one you could work
with – otherwise after a day handling
anything up to 100 tons of cargo they'd
just be bleeding, red, raw and blis-
tered'. Still, accompanying the display
is the ticket recording how one docker
had to resort to pawning his hook in
1911, for 4d – just a few pence. The
museum has dealt imaginatively with
the decline of the docks, with a tableau
of George's last ride from Alan Bleas-
dale's play, *The Boys from the Blackstuff.*

John Everett Millais, Isabella, *1849*

real world, can easily become quite a regular pattern on the surface of a flat picture.

Look at the 'Christ Discovered by his Parents in the Temple', painted by Simone Martini in 1342. Pictures of this period tended to use pattern very explicitly. This one is unusual for its period because of the intensity of the human narrative combined with the decorative effect. Joseph is affectionate, yet angry at the worry Jesus has caused his parents. 'When did you last see your Mother?', he seems to be saying reproachfully. (What he actually is saying appears in the Latin inscription on the painting.) Much of the narrative is in the faces, but the body language of the figures has to be conveyed by drapery patterns as artists at this time did not construct figures anatomically. The zig-zag hems and hanging corners of the draperies have been turned into a repeating pattern, in a surface that is all pattern.

Nicolas Poussin's 'Landscape with the Ashes of Phocion' is much more illusionistic. The landscape is idealised, but the way that, for instance, the slanting sunlight just catches the tops of the crags is reminiscent of moments we can all remember in landscapes. There are wonderful patterns here too, in the foliage of the large tree to the right. The irregular shape of the outline of each little cluster of leaves is

David Hockney, Peter getting out of Nick's pool, *1967*

repeated on a larger scale in the shape of the foliage on each bow, then repeated again in the profile of the foliage as a whole.

The Victorian John Brett's paintings are so detailed that the illusion of realism disguises the way that he groups things of different kinds, so as to make the surface of his pictures as patterned as the most finely-woven carpet. In 'The Stone-Breaker', look at the pile of large stones awaiting hammering. They have the gently curving profiles, sharp corners and smooth surfaces of flints broken open. Painted as a pile, these shapes make an extraordinary patch of patterning, contrasting with the liquid flow-lines of the dead tree above them.

By contrast, in Dame Laura Knight's 'Spring in Saint John's Wood' it is not so much the shape of things represented that make the pattern (though the wind-blown leaves on the central tree do provide a repeating motif) as the shapes of the paint strokes

making them up. This trend becomes very obvious in some of the other later, 20th century pictures, such as David Bomberg's 'Mount St. Hilarion', whose whole surface is covered in a carpet of huge brush strokes, with a pattern on a smaller scale left behind by the wriggling hairs of the brush with which they were applied.

Those brush-stroke patterns only show up because oil paint is often not applied smooth and flat, but with a pronounced three-dimensional texture. Many artists use the texture not just to make patterns, but to help represent their subject. This is something else to look out for in paintings of any period. But all too often in older paintings the relief texture has been squashed or rubbed away by the harsh conservation procedures of earlier times. An 18th century painting with a relatively undamaged surface, therefore, is a rare treasure. To see what oil paint should look like, go to Arthur Devis's portrait of 'Mr. and Mrs.

Rembrandt, Self-portrait, *c.1629*

Atherton'. Devis's technique was so sound that his paintings have rarely suffered much. Notice the paint of Mr. Atherton's silk waistcoat: below the pocket, the little ridges of paint still have sharp edges. The lace design of Mrs. Atherton's collar can be seen to have been lifted out of wet paint with the end of the paintbrush, leaving just a tiny recess whose edges still show relief.

Another transformation that sometimes happens in the paint surface is less obtrusive, and can be especially fascinating. With time, layers of oil paint become more transparent. Areas painted out by an artist can put in a ghostly reappearance. Look for instance at Jacob van Schuppen's 'Guitar Player'. On the left is a little dancing girl. The artist has changed the position of her raised right arm, and its original position now just shows through. The effect of transparency can be so expressive that in one case in the Walker it may even have been created deliberately. In the background of Ercole di Roberti's 'Lamentation over the Dead Christ' is a scene of the crucifixion. The horizon line can now be seen through all the figures. A little to the right of the right-hand cross, are there two figures standing, or just one? A little to the left, another ghost has 'reappeared' at the foot of a pointing figure, in the foreground.

Portrait of a Lady with a Parrot, *French School, c.1530*

MACCLESFIELD

Macclesfield Silk Museum

Heritage Centre, Roe Street,
Macclesfield SK11 6UT
(0625) 613210

and

Paradise Mill Museum

Old Park Lane, Macclesfield
Silk Museum closed Sunday mornings and all day Monday; Paradise Mill closed every morning and all day Mondays; open Bank Holiday Mondays. 🚻 ▣

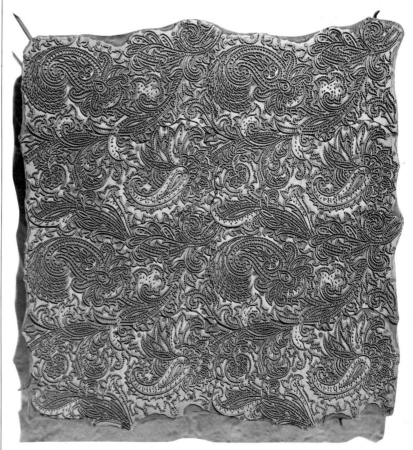

A block used in block printing

 W: chair lift to basement of Silk Museum.
🛏 book through Public Services Manager. ⚲ must book: contact Education Officer; out of hours visits possible by arrangement.

A single ticket admits visitors to two sites, within a few moments walk of one another. On the ground floor and in the cellars of the Silk Museum is a documentary display, with artefacts, audio-visual display and information panels, chronicling the story of the silk industry in Macclesfield. On the top floor of nearby Paradise Mill is the real thing, a working museum, based on looms left just as they were when the last hand-loom silk operation in town stopped trading in 1981.

The display in the Silk Museum

provides the background for the visit to the Mill. To the left of the entrance lobby an exhibition recalls the history of the Sunday School that houses the Silk Museum. Its centrepiece is a model, of 1813, showing the whole building, with its two top floors given over to one large assembly room, used for services and teaching. This was a Sunday School that with difficulty kept itself independent of any particular religious sect. Victorian values were its staple. Regular attenders earned Cards of Honour, each inscribed: 'A man may be great by chance, but never wise or good without taking pains for it.' Sunday school attenders, presumably, were not interested in being just rich, rather than great, wise or good.

A staircase, hung with pictures showing the life cycle of the silk-moth, leads down to the main sequence of displays. The history of silk goes back thousands of years in China, and Chinese silk was imported for use in medieval English embroidery. Macclesfield cornered the market early in silk buttons, wound by cottagers around wooden templates, for distant agents who also imported the thread. There were buttons for every walk of life, and Macclesfield thrived. Gradually, entrepreneurs introduced to the town first the throwing, or twisting, of their own thread from raw silk, for transport to the weavers of Spitalfields, and then introduced weaving as well. It became a great industry, but always a vulnerable one, as wars and trade laws alternately protected then exposed it to foreign competition. This much we learn in a first roomful of panels, and then in a multi-screen audio-visual presentation.

A succession of rooms full of pattern books, reconstructions and panels of information fill in the details. There is a large model, still only one third the size of the original, of the giant cylindrical machines that mechanised the delicate throwing process, and a small model, set in motion with a push-button, of a power loom. A reconstruction of a block-maker's workspace, complete with chest of tools, is the centrepiece for the display of printing. Early blocks were relief patterns

Membership certificate of the Amalgamated Society of Dyers

gouged out of wood. The latest held the dye on an intricate tracery of metal, cast in fine grooves and pits burned into a wooden surface. Designs like these, the displays remind us, were the fruit of training, in the art colleges founded to bring the manufactures of England, including silk, to the point where they could compete with the elevated taste of the French. There is plenty of technical detail, from Jacquard's brilliant invention, perfected by 1804, of a loom that could be

programmed to weave the most intricate different patterns with punched cards, to William Perkin's aniline dyes. The story comes into the recent past with the industry's specialised contributions during the Second World War. Parachutes were made of silk, and although artificial threads had to be used for some production after 1943, it could only be for bomber crews: only silk would pack tightly enough for the restricted space of fighter cockpits. Even more exotically,

1   Greek icon of Virgin and Child Enthroned, *c.1800. Blackburn Museum and Art Gallery, Blackburn (Lewis Collection).*

2 *above* Toy shop front,
English, c.1940. Warrington
Museum and Art Gallery,
Warrington.

3 *right* Cased glass scent bottle
with painted and gilt decoration,
English, 19th century. Harris
Museum and Art Gallery,
Preston (French Collection).

4 *opposite, top left*
Reconstruction of a section of the
priory church floor, c.1325.
Norton Priory Museum,
Runcorn.

5 *opposite, top right*
Marquetry panel on an
ebonised, inlaid Dundee
cabinet, made by Gillows,
c.1872. Judges' Lodgings
Museum, Lancaster.

6 *opposite* Interior of a
showman's living wagon of
1912. The British Commercial
Vehicle Museum, Leyland.

7   *Kirifuri Fall, Kurokami Mountain, Shimotsuke Province*, a Japanese woodblock print by Hokusai, c.1833. *Manchester City Art Gallery, Manchester.*

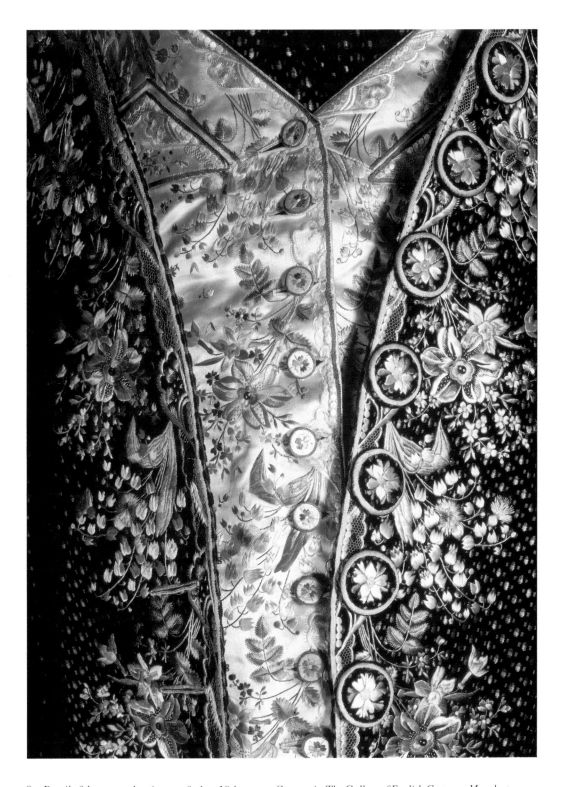

8   *Detail of the coat and waistcoat of a late 18th century Court suit. The Gallery of English Costume, Manchester.*

9   *Dove Cottage, from the garden.*
Dove Cottage, and the Grasmere
and Wordsworth Museum,
Grasmere.

10 opposite   Longcase clock made
by Symcocke of Prescot, 1775, with
astronomical faces at the top.
Prescot Museum, Prescot.

11 opposite, top right   Janice
Tchalenko, Red Bowl, *1985.*
Bolton Museum and Art Gallery,
Bolton.

12 opposite, bottom right
Braithwaite motorcycle in the
mechanic's workshop. Museum of
Lakeland Life and Industry,
Kendal.

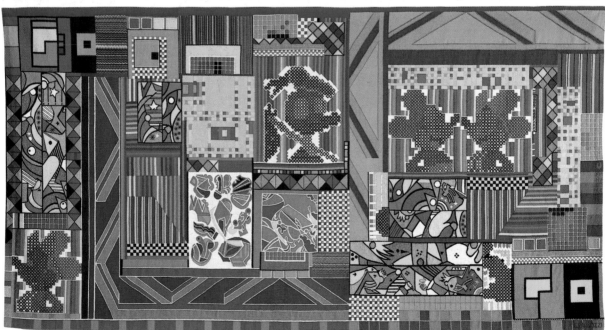

13 top   The 'Worcester' and 'Gifford' canal boats. The Boat Museum, Ellesmere Port.

14 above   The Whitworth Tapestry, 1968, designed by Eduardo Paolozzi and woven by the Edinburgh Tapestry Company. The Whitworth Art Gallery, Manchester.

squares of silk, which could be discreetly slipped into the smallest space,
offered the ideal base for secret maps,
for escapees or agents.

A short walk down the road, and a
few flights of stairs, bring us to the
place where Messrs Cartwright and
Sheldon took over a set of looms,
already old in 1912, and ran them till
1981. The twenty-six hand looms at
Paradise Mill are all that remains of the
six thousand once in Macclesfield, and
through a window you may have
pointed out to you one of the rows of
cottages that would once have housed a
frame in nearly every attic. The
wooden framework for the machines
runs right down the room. The looms
are beautiful, intricate, yet held
together with linkages of cord and
systems of knots to allow just the right
balance of tensions. Some are ordinary, shaft looms, of the kind those
cottage attics would have held, but the
stars are the Jacquards. Only they
could cope with intricate patterns in
nearly 12,000 threads, which it took to
make up the silk squares, just twenty-
eight inches wide, that became the
speciality here, for the tie trade. The
machines are explained well in cap-
tions, but can usually be seen working,
with a guide to point out a wealth of
detail. Nowhere else can you see and
hear so vividly just how these astonishing ancestors of the computer
worked.

Weaving consists of warp threads
running lengthwise, criss-crossed by
weft threads. A loom is essentially an
array of warp threads – as many as
11,520 in some cases – running
lengthwise along the loom. The warp
threads have to be separated into two
groups, above and below, to allow the
shuttle, which guides the weft thread,
through from one side to the other.
The patterns woven depend on which
warp threads are raised or lowered for
each pass of the shuttle. Not many
variations are possible with an ordinary, shaft loom, but the variety is
endless with the Jacquard. In this
machine, warp threads are attached to
harness cords, which in turn are
grouped onto hooks; the hooks are on
rods that can be raised or lowered by

Reconstruction of a block-engraving workshop

View of the looms in Paradise Mill

treadle motion, raising or lowering, in
turn, the warp threads attached. Each
time the treadle is pressed a different
set of hooks is raised, their selection
controlled by a needle and punch-card
system – hence the computer connec-
tion. There is one punch card for each
weft thread in the design. The weaver
works the Jacquard mechanism by
operating the treadle with his foot, the
frame and shuttle with his hands, and
may have to operate a lever too, to
select at high speed one of up to four
shuttles, each with a different colour of
thread for the weft. It is heavy work,
and the mechanism slams the punched
cards into the forest of needles that
crown the machine with a noise like an

army coming to attention. Yet a skilled
weaver could produce some fifteen
yards of silk a week, at 200 threads to
the inch. The threading of the machine
was also a specialist task, taking an
expert team several days.

Finally, just off the workshop, is a
little room in which the designer, with
the aid of complicated tables, translated his inventions into the code of
punched holes, and made the concerti-
nas of cards that you see at the top of
the Jacquards, each one prepared in a
large, specialised punching machine.
Next door is the office from which the
business was run, with its furniture
intact, an invoice ready to be completed in the typewriter.

MANCHESTER

The Gallery of English Costume

*Platt Hall, Platt Fields, Rusholme,
Manchester M14 5LL*
(061) 224 5217
Closed Sunday mornings and all
day Tuesday. 🄵 🄿
♿ S: wheelchair access to ground
floor only.
🚺 & 🚹 phone museum to book,
and Manchester Galleries
Education Service (061 236 9422)
for details of services.
Library and archive: access by
appointment.

Many museums have followed where
the Gallery of English Costume led,
since it was established in 1947 with
the collection of the costume historian,
Dr C. Willett Cunnington. But it has
kept its lead as the finest costume
collection in the north of England, and
is one of the largest in Britain, containing around 18,000 items. In one sense,
its pioneering role leaves it at a temporary disadvantage. Some more recent foundations have resolved happier
solutions to the problems of displaying

Man's buff linen doublet, 1625–35

Original publicity photograph for the Cotton Board's 1955 Exhibition of Woven Cotton Dress Fabrics, Manchester, showing an evening coat by Owen of Lachasse

costume in a period house than were
available when Platt Hall was fitted out
with showcases. The surviving
architecture of the interior, however,
compensates for this. From a pillared,
stone-flagged lobby we ascend either
arm of a curving staircase with delicate
balustrade, set in an oval stairwell. The
pillars and arch of the upstairs landing
echo the pillared lobby below.

Costume is physically hard to preserve. Most of anything that survives to
enter our museums is dress for special
occasions and 'best', and on the whole
for women. Everyday and working
clothes were generally worn out, and
rarely kept. Once in a museum, fabrics
still quickly fade and rot if exhibited for
long, so costume displays are changed
as often as possible, and only very

'The Dandy's Toilet', c.1820

subdued lighting is used.

Upstairs at Platt Hall when I visited, were, in one of the galleries, day dresses and accessories of the mid to late 19th century. They showed the endless imagination exercised in adding to basic shapes some trimming of lace, tassles or feathery plush. At the opposite end of the first floor, a corridor showed fashion plates, and caricatures of earlier styles. A tableau nearby displayed women's wear around the house, together with a sewing table, reminding you that fashionable dress was like a theatrical performance, requiring small armies of staff to do the grind that kept up appearances.

A third room upstairs contains great rarities, embroidered garments and accessories from before 1750. In the age of Shakespeare the established man of the world retired to bed in a night cap, not the kind with a long floppy point familiar from ghost stories, but a small, tight-fitting affair, with just a little pointed dome. Usually, they were most delicately embroidered, with relief patterns in thread all of one colour, or with dense decorations of creatures and flowers. Both kinds are on show here. There are also jackets for men and women of the kind seen in the portraits of Van Dyck, with soft contours in voluminous fabric gleam-

Evening dress & matching cloak of emerald green silk brocade, made by Jay's, London, 1912

ing with metallic thread in twisting plant-stem patterns. There is a doll with alternative costumes of 1740 or so in here, amongst other, smaller early items.

Downstairs, the gallery at one end of the building had a display of the printed dresses that made cotton a fashionable fabric again in the late 1940s and 1950s, after a century of relegation to the everyday. Platt Hall has a special collection of these, so that many of the designers who dominated the industry are represented. The inventions of Pierre Cardin, Hardie Amies and Michael Sherard for different years, for example, could thus be compared. A display nearby when I visited offered a striking contrast: vivid embroideries of both Hindu and Muslim herder and warrior societies of Northern India and Pakistan. The embroideries were major possessions of these peoples, and immense effort went into their intricate patterns and rich colours.

They seemed to me to offer a vigorous reproach to the costumes of the fashionable western world of the 1920s

Pink figured silk dress, c.1780–90

and '30s, which were on show at the opposite end of the building. It is not that expense was spared on these svelte and tubular numbers, but that they exude an overwhelming air of blasé weariness. They certainly compete with the Asian costumes in terms of the varieties of sequins and metallic fragments stitched into them, or trailing languidly from them. A 'Cocktail Time' tableau was particularly effective. One lady, in lime green with fawn-pink silk gauze, dangled a tiny bag, or purse, just about the size and shape of a large yo-yo; its modernistic lines were softened by tassles, to make it more feminine.

Nearby downstairs there was a stylishly presented exhibition on knitting, but I was particularly taken by a fascinating room revealing the intimate secrets of corsets and stays, which held a vice-like (and often harmful) grip on the waists of women, and for short periods men, in the past. An early corset, displayed inside out and unlined, showed the fearsome array of whalebone strips that did the gripping, each in a little sewn compartment. Steel, then elastic, replaced the whalebone, but still the advertising had always to sell an awkward combination of rigid restraint mixed with assurances of unfettered suppleness. 'See how they bend', promise little slogans in the corners of the box of a steel corset of 1900. Letters in the form of an endless spring introduce the item as the Apollo, 'delightfully flexible' and 'perfectly pliable'; the corset itself has 'SPARTAN' steel supports. The corset come-back of the 1950s depended on drowning the severity in clouds of fantasy femininity: 'The new figure in fashion – a strapless corset that keeps your bosom high and rounded as it flattens and elongates your torso. Feminine as French perfume in petal-light nylon net and nylon voile.' It probably lit up the room with static electric sparks as you slid into it, like a *femme fatale* putting on armour.

The museum has an extensive library and archive of books, magazines, fashion plates and photographs, which is available to students and researchers in the costume field, by appointment.

Greater Manchester Museum of Science and Industry

Liverpool Road, Castlefield, Manchester M3 4JP
(061) 832 2244
Open daily. 🚻 🖼 🅿
♿ **ST**: access good to most parts, but no wheelchair access to 'Underground Manchester' and parts of 'National Electricity Gallery'.
♿ & ♿ phone Education Service (061 833 0027) to book and for information about services.

Science museums used to tend to consist of a row of steam engines, some weird instruments in cabinets, and one or two buttons to press, to make the wheels of models go round. Manchester's new version, first opened in 1983, claims to be Europe's fastest growing example of a new generation. The steam engines here comprise Europe's largest collection, lovingly tended so that they are often to be seen in action. But now there is also much more to see, especially the National Electricity Gallery, displays of the nitty gritty of Manchester history above and below

One of Stella's brass microscopes

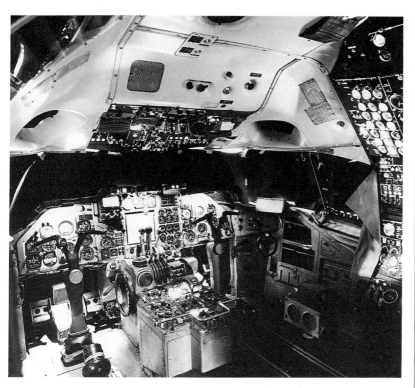

The flight deck of a Trident

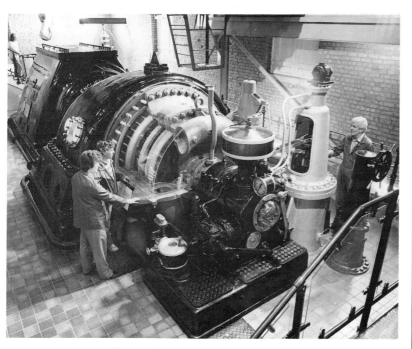

An engine in the Power Hall

ground, and a huge hall of air and space machines. You can talk to engineers as they operate machines, watch videos, and above all try out exhibits for yourself. Best of all, there is a new 'Xperiment' gallery, in which you can explore the principles of pure science by playing with amazing, spectacular and puzzling demonstrations. The museum is steadily developing these displays and others through the historic buildings of a huge site, which includes the world's first railway passenger station and first railway warehouse. There is more to see now than can easily be absorbed on a single visit. As a bonus, there are tantalising glimpses of the neighbouring Granada Television studios.

A visit begins in the Lower Byrom Street Warehouse. Recent renovation has made the most of its fine cast-iron pillars and beams, with a brilliantly bright decor including a chic gradual ramp to make exploration easy. 'Xperiment' is on the second floor. Amongst a hive of noisy activities you can watch your reflection change as you bend a bendy mirror, freeze your own shadow on a wall, or examine the thinnest sheet in the world – a sheet of soapy water several feet high, glittering in streaming irridescent colours. Downstairs in the warehouse are historic textile machines, everything from cottage spinning wheels to machines as big as a room. Especially intriguing is the Jacquard loom, an ancestor of the computer though it was invented 200 years ago. The arrangements of threads, which determine the pattern of the fabric, are controlled by giant punched cards, fed into the top of the machine one by one from a concertina of dozens of the cards. From this display a passage leads past wood and metalworking machines, and an overview of the museum's own workshops, to the back of the warehouse.

A short walk down steps and past the cast-iron columns of an 1880s railway viaduct brings you to the National Electricity Gallery. To call it a gallery is something of an understatement. It is a four storey building, with a huge steam turbine in the middle of it. The turbine was one of six in a Bolton

Turbine Hall of the Electricity Gallery

power station of the 1920s, and we enter the display by passing right through the middle of one of the condensers. The passage through which we pass has been cut through a forest of thin pipes, which channelled cold water to cool the steam, exhausted from the work of turning the turbine, until it condensed back to water. There are plenty of technical details in the gallery, presented through videos, models and push-button models. There are also some of the best (at the time of writing) historic furnished rooms in Manchester – kitchens and living-rooms full of electrical appliances of the 1930s and '50s. A display about the history of computers, in which Manchester played a major early role, is here too; the early circuitry on show looks colossally clumsy. Here are also modern computer quizzes to try.

From Electricity, a tunnel leads to the entrance to the historic Liverpool Road Station, the first passenger railway station in the world. On the ground floor you can follow 'The Making of Manchester' story and down in the basement is 'Underground Manchester'. Sewers are a subject of special concern to Mancunians, whose streets intermittently collapse into them. This display explains why, and provides a full-scale reconstruction of a sewer for you to stroll down. Mind the dangling fronds. It also presents a reconstruction of a Roman legionaries' latrine; a trip there was nothing if not a social occasion for the guardians of the Empire, it would appear. Watch the

Walk-through reconstruction of a Manchester sewer

hypnotic motion of the Victorian 'Tippler' toilet, too: it flushed automatically from time to time, fed economically by waste water from the kitchen sink, just the thing for the working classes. Richer folk could enjoy the more wasteful flushed toilet, of which there are elegantly encased early specimens here. Upstairs in these buildings there is a reconstruction of the original first class ticket office, and, on the first floor, displays of historic microscopes and cameras.

Heading back towards the southern end of the site, you will come to the Power Hall, full of steam locomotives and static engines, some of the latter generally performing magisterially, with slow graceful movements of their giant pistons and huge wheels. If you have ever wondered what was inside those Thomas the Tank Engine-type locomotives, with the lump in the middle like a dromedary, this is your chance. 'Pender', an engine of 1873 from the Isle of Wight, has been opened up, to show all the pipes and valves. This also is your chance to climb up and try to work out the forest of levers and taps, which the driver on the footplate of a locomotive had to know his way around. Especially grand specimens were supplied for the exotic mountain landscapes of the Empire.

Finally, across the road is another whole museum, the Air and Space Gallery, set in a magnificent iron-frame market hall. It is full of airplanes, rockets and a few satellites. My favourite was the nose of a Trident which only went out of British Airways' service on the Manchester shuttle in 1985. The flight deck, upstairs, is fun, but have a good look downstairs at the one landing wheel still attached. At the back of it is a lever, which someone could climb down into the bowels of the aeroplane to release if the wheel refused to drop down otherwise when wanted. Reassuring? They do not say how often it was needed. I also liked the replica of the Triplane in which A.V. Roe – 'Roe the Hopper' to his friends (because his flights tended to be on the short side) finally stunned them all with the first English sustained flight, in June 1908.

Manchester City Art Gallery

Mosley Street, Manchester M2 3JL
(061) 236 9422
Open daily. ◨ ▣
& **S**: wheelchair access very limited.
▯ & ▯ phone Education Service for details of services. ◉

Manchester City Art Gallery is a gilded treasure chest with feet of clay. The gilded bit is the suite of first floor galleries, renovated in recent years to give it a High Victorian look. The gallery ceilings and cornices are a restless confection of gold, red, green and cream classical revival motifs. They cap a world-class collection of European pictures, which begins with a crucifixion attributed to the 13th century master Duccio, ends with Max Ernst and David Hockney, and includes one of the finest groups of Pre-Raphaelite pictures anywhere. One of the feet of clay on the ground floor is a spiritual one, a display about the down to earth L.S. Lowry. The other is literally clay, an outstanding collection of English and oriental ceramics. There are also good Dutch pictures, English silverware and glass downstairs.

The hugely popular L.S. Lowry was an artist of the people. On loan here from the Lowry Estate are the contents of the rooms he mostly lived in, his parlour and studio, presented in faithful reconstructions. A photograph of the artist in his parlour enables us to see how faithful the reconstructions are, whilst listening to tapes of friends recalling him, and Lowry himself giving a quite wonderfully crusty but warm interview to Roy Cross of BBC Radio Manchester in 1972. A friend recalls that visitors and artists had almost to lie in the chairs to avoid being impaled on the springs, and so we see him in the photo. Drawing pins held up the anaglypta paper on the ceiling, and there was no shade on the light. The heavy oak furniture, in the Victorian Jacobean style, was inherited from his parents. Lowry himself added to his mother's collection of clocks, until he had fourteen, and loved them as companions, 'real friends, oh dear me yes'. He bought pictures too, with a special fascination for the women of Rossetti, '... really rather horrible – but I'm fascinated by them'. Mr. Lowry, as he was known to his friends, seems to have been torn between affection and loathing for the area that gave him his subjects. He certainly could not imagine why he had bought the horrible house he so steadfastly neglected, and declares in the interview that he is sick of the whole area. But he loved the people: 'I feel more strongly about these people than I ever did about the industrial scene. They are real people, sad people. I'm attracted to sadness, and there are some very sad things. I feel like them.' It is all there in the drawings that accompany the reconstructions. One or two are from the 1920s, pre-dating his familiar work, but already show a rare ability to give a soul to a figure only slightly drawn.

Much of the early ceramics downstairs are as down-to-earth as a Lowry painting. The early English earthenwares, especially, make no great pretence at refinement. One mid-17th century one is piously inscribed: 'FAST AND PRAY AND PETTE

The Tatton Cup, c.1760

[pity] THE POOR/AMEND THY LIFE AND SINNE NO MORE.' They did no such thing, of course, and a jug of a century later is closer to the horrid heart of old England. It is one of a number in the form of a bear chained for baiting, for public amusement. It holds a captured victim, looking suspiciously like the preacher of virtue and abstinence John Wesley, and to add insult to injury, his mouth has been widened so that the end of the drinker's clay pipe may be rested in it.

Many of the things on display, however, might have been bought with an eye to a bit of gentle social one-upmanship. Who, for instance, bought the paintings of peasants, like the 17th century one here, by Isaac Ostade, of a woman trying to separate two fighting men in a huge, raftered barn? Did pictures like these appeal to the countryfolk they represented, or were they bought by people who wanted to look down on the clownishness of the peasants? We certainly know, from the diary of Samuel Pepys, that English silverware of the later 17th century could be bought partly as an investment, but also very much to astonish the dinner guests. That did not stop the period from being a high point of simplicity in the design of these wares, with effects depending on shape rather than decoration, which continued for the first decades of the 18th century. Manchester's collection is especially strong in quite rare items of this period, though with some ornate later examples offering a contrast.

Themes of popularity and refinement appear in the room of oriental wares, too. The ceramics, including some grave wares over 2,000 years old, are exclusive. The porcelains are exquisitely fine bodied. But on the walls are early 19th century Japanese prints, considered so vulgar by Japanese connoisseurs when they were produced that it is claimed they first came to the West as packing in crates of ceramics. Nonetheless, wonderful artists worked for this popular market, none more so than Hokusai, and he made no finer print than 'Kirifuri Waterfall' in this display (colour plate 7). It is a festival of patterns adding up to an image in a way Western artists could not attempt.

Upstairs in the main picture galleries, work, idleness and class are the subjects to which the attention of the viewer is drawn by one of the most startling of the many major Pre-Raphaelite paintings in the collection, 'Work' by Ford Maddox Brown. Lift a rather plush-looking cloth (it looks like some untouchable historic item, but is there to protect from light) on the case below the picture to see preliminary sketches and the artist's explanations. It is 1850 or so. A scene of road-works in Hampstead provides an opportunity to show a selection of navvies, described by the artist as if they were in a museum typological display, including one real corker, 'in the prime of manly health and beauty'. They are watched by notable brain workers. The scene is also crowded with persons of equivocal status, such as a purely decorative idle woman and a hopeless case, a chickweed seller who, the explanatory leaflet says, was 'never *taught to work*'. There's one horrid incident, at the extreme right. 'A policeman has caught an orange girl in the offence of resting her basket on a post, and himself adminis-

Attributed to Duccio, The Crucifixion, *1278–1318*

Ford Madox Brown, Work, *1852–65*

Ancient Egyptian tomb figure of a duck

Slipware charger by Thomas Toft, c.1670

Manchester Jewish Museum

190 Cheetham Hill Road, Manchester M8 8LW
(061) 834 9879/832 7353
Closed on Fridays, Saturdays and Jewish holidays. 🅶
♿ S: wheelchair access to ground floor only (main part of synagogue and temporary exhibition area); stairs to upper floor.
🚻 & 🍴 must book in advance; evening bookings possible when staffing allows.

The first Jews to settle in Manchester, as the displays in the Manchester Jewish Museum explain, were families of pedlars who established businesses in the town in the later 18th century. Others soon followed, and the great Nathan Mayer Rothschild spent the first decade of the 19th century here as a textile merchant. Unlike the majority of the waves of later jewish immigrants to the city, many of the earliest settlers were not Ashkenazim – Jews from Central or Eastern Europe – but Sephardim, Jews of Spanish and Portuguese origin. By the third quarter of the 19th century the Sephardim represented a prosperous group of some thirty families in a total jewish population of around 5,000. They opened in 1874 their own small synagogue, Moorish in style and lavishly decorated. It was re-opened as a museum of the whole community in 1984, with treasured possessions, archival material, devotional furnishings and equipment, and recordings of reminiscences. The museum now has an active educational programme, and besides the permanent displays there are temporary exhibitions. Subjects have included 'Jewish Weddings' and 'Immigrant Trades and Skills'. The exhibition at the time of writing is 'City and Community, Jewish Enterprise in the Manchester Economy 1788–1988'.

The main room of the synagogue is a raftered hall, built to accommodate a congregation of 200 men on the ground floor, and 100 women on a

ters justice in the shape of a push, that sends her fruit all over the road.' Now, just where did the artist stand on all this? Lift another cloth opposite to reveal the meaning of Holman Hunt's picture of rustics mucking about with a death's-head moth. Bet you never guess what the picture is about otherwise in a million years.

The gallery entrance hall still sometimes looks a bit like an embassy into which one should not have wandered, but do not be deterred. Nowadays, upstairs and downstairs, the gallery warms the faintly daunting splendour of its decor with innovative attempts to make art more approachable. A blue, man-sized, sphinx-like sculpture by Dhruva Mistry greeted visitors taking one route through the upper galleries on my visit, and beside it, appropriately a little more than man-size, was a tower of exultant women by sculptress Christine Kowal Post. Downstairs a more earnest display explained terms like 'rococo' and 'baroque'. More of this kind of thing is in the pipeline. In the Athenaeum next door the gallery holds temporary exhibitions, mostly of contemporary art, but with intermittent shows of international importance.

The family of Russian shoemaker Eli Weitz of Chernigor, c.1908

to by lifting telephone handsets at numerous points in the display. There are particularly haunting mementoes of life in the Czarist Russian Empire from which many Jews fled. Strong faces and intense eyes stare out from photographs of bearded elders and family groups, in the peasant clothing of central Europe. One voice on the phone recalls leaving Vilna, in Lithuania, at the age of twelve, because there was no way for a Jew to make a living there. Another recalls an attack by cossacks in Odessa, and the sight of a man being shot dead. England promised better. The father of one speaker heard of the visit to the Czar, to plead for protection for Jews, made by the distinguished Victorian English Jew and tireless roving diplomat for his people, Sir Moses Montefiore. 'If a Jew can be a lord in England,' the father remarked, 'that's where I'm going'.

balcony on three sides of the hall. At the time of its renovation as a museum, tests were done to discover the original decorative scheme, and it has been followed as much as possible in the present decoration of beige, green and gold. The metalwork of railings around different areas displays a variety of Moorish patterning. The overall effect is harmonious, with rich, glowing stained glass adding touches of intensity. The windows down the sides of the hall are emblematic representations of incidents from the Old Testament. The subject of each window is associated with the biblical figure whose name was borne by the member of the community commemorated by the window. Thus a window, for example, that commemorates Moses Lisbona shows the Burning Bush of the Biblical Moses. The great round window at the east end of the synagogue presents the Menora, the seven-branched candlestick in the Temple in Jerusalem, along with other emblems of the faith.

The synagogue is dominated by an elaborate cupboard at the east end of the Hall, and a railed platform at the west end, on which is a lectern. Both are principally for the preservation and proper use of the Scrolls of the Law, the Torah. The cupboard is the Ark, in which the scrolls were kept, and the platform is the Tebah, from which they were read. A Torah scroll is displayed on the lectern, along with the special pointer, or Yad, which the reader used to scan it. It is inscribed with the five books of Moses, known as the Pentateuch, which are the first books of the Hebrew bible. A small section of scroll is unwound at a time between two tall spools, like a film in a camera. The scrolls used in services must be in perfect condition. The ones that we see can be used in the museum because they have with time become 'possul', unfit for sacred use. Between services, the scrolls were kept in the Ark in their velvet mantles. Saphardi Jews sometimes mounted the scrolls in metal-covered wooden cases. One of each is displayed in the Ark here.

The historical displays are on the balcony. The photographs, documents and reconstructions are brought to life by reminiscences, which we may listen

Sephardi case for a Scroll of the Law

Exterior view of the museum

It was no promised land. A large map shows the geography of Jewish settlement in Manchester, and voices on the 'phones alongside recall the sharp distinctions between rich and poor within the community. The wealthy Sephardim and Ashkenazim lived near the Sephardi Synagogue, or the Great Synagogue down the road. The poorest districts were Redbank and Strangeways. 'They were very remote ... we couldn't speak a word of Yiddish.' 'It smelled ... the smell of Redbank was terrible.' Other displays present the discipline, education and industriousness of the community. There is a reconstruction of a kitchen parlour in a modest home in 1896, with the table prepared for the Sabbath Eve. The wine is kosher and nothing if not international. With a mixed Spanish and French name, Alicante Superieur, it came from Palestine. Some Jews did very well. Samuel Claff beams contentedly and prosperously from his photograph, one of those Russian immigrants who became established as 'Alrightniks'. Another reconstruction presents a corner of a water-proof garment workshop in the 1930s. The Jewish community joined in the good thing that Manchester made of vulcanised rainwear. Even so, things were still hard for many of the new wave of immigrants from Nazi Germany in this era. As the displays record, children found refuge, but many adults faced internment in the early years of the Second World War. Meanwhile fellow Jews in Palestine at the time were liable to be confronted by the 'Declaration of Faith in Palestine Victory' on display

here: 'I solemnly hereby declare my unshakeable faith in a British Victory bringing freedom to all the peoples of this earth ...'

Other displays present vignettes of the more humdrum life of the community, its charities and hospitals, its leaders and their disputes. A particular bone of contention was the degree of control exercised on Manchester Jewry from London. Spice was added to the dispute because upon it hung the question of whether fees for licensing special traders came to the Manchester community and its leaders, or went south. 'Listen Dear Jews', begins a notice distributed by the great Manchester Rabbi Joseph Jaffe in the 1890s, displayed here and translated for us; 'Take no notice of the ban by which this Dr. Adler and his Beth Din prohibit the meat which is under my supervision ... The meat ... is strictly kosher ... and my shocket is not a profaner of the Sabbath, but a pious Jew, and also a good slaughterer ... I declare null and void, like the dust of the earth and like a broken shard, the ban by Dr. Adler ...' But there were entertainments too, commemorated here by a collection of posters and leaflets, like the one for Molly Picon in 'Yiddle with his Fiddle', an all-Jewish comedy with subtitles in English, at the Riviera Cinema in the 1930s.

Sephardi scribe's silver reed-holder

The Manchester Museum

University of Manchester,
Oxford Road, Manchester M13 9PL
(061) 275 2634
Closed Sundays. ▣
♿ S: wheelchair access limited.
▯ & ▯ must book: phone Education Service (061 275 2631) to book and for information about extensive services. ◎

The collections of the Manchester Museum are set in an attractive maze of galleries, bridges and balconies, built between 1888 and 1927 by three generations of architects from the Waterhouse family. They hide behind a fine Victorian gothic façade, in turn embedded in the august main buildings of Manchester University. In a room within this very group of buildings, Rutherford first split the atom. But do not let the pompous surroundings and their burden of learning put you off. Nobody, wandering through the halls and galleries of Manchester Museum, can escape the Big Questions, about Life, Man and the Universe, whether you reckon to ponder them till you have got the whole thing worked out, or just wonder at them. Thousands of objects, man-made and natural, selected from huge collections of national importance, present vivid glimpses of the evolution of the world, and of the many different ways in which people have tried to come to terms with it, practically and spiritually. Geology sets the scene, Botany and Zoology bring it to life, and Archaeology and Ethnography populate it, with artefacts and human remains from the urban cultures of the Mediterranean and South America, and forest cultures from all over the world. You can get an insight into daily life in ancient Egypt, watch live animals in the aquarium, or count the rings in a section through a tree-trunk that was already 500 years old when William the Conqueror won the Battle of Hastings.

All the galleries are to the left of the Entrance Hall. The first room often houses temporary exhibitions. Lindow Man, recovered from peaty ground in Cheshire, was here in one recent show, and others extend the treatment of every aspect of the museum's collections. Beyond it on the ground floor is Geology, with minerals showing a symmetry of design reflecting their crystalline formation. An alternative route leads upstairs from the entrance hall to the Ethnology displays, and the recently remodelled Egyptology galleries.

Here, a first room shows artefacts of daily life in ancient Egypt, whilst awaiting you in the second are the spectacular mummies and coffin cases (ill. on cover). The scientific unwrapping and study of the mummies has become a Manchester speciality. It starts with something like a surgical operation, involving a number of standard techniques of high-tech medical examination, but may take a team of scientists many hours. Their findings turn the mummified figures into real people, such as Asru, who lived 2,500 years ago. Poor Asru. She was infested with worms, suffered severe ear infection, a slipped disc, nasty dental problems, fused bones in an infected finger joint, arterial disease and cancer. And she was a member of the privileged classes.

A staircase in Egyptology offers you the choice of going up to special collections of archery, oriental art and (being reorganised at the time of writing) Mediterranean antiquities. Otherwise, a passage brings you through to a large collection of mammals (look for the enchanting Cape Jumping Hare), and another staircase takes you up to the comprehensive bird collections. Here you can identify any bird you are likely to have seen in your garden, find out all about feathers, or whether birds really have hollow bones. You can also sit in a booth and listen to bird song. A press-button enables you to start two programmes of recordings, of about four minutes each. You can hear the strange, melancholy but weirdly metallic clang of the South American Bell Bird, listen to Great Northern Divers warbling to one another, amazingly like Bizet's pearl fishers, be jeered at by the manic Laughing Jackass and listen to the dawn chorus. Strange to think that

Leaf insect, Phyllium crurifolium

Children with the 'hippo' mammal anatomy information exhibit

Greek red-figure amphora by the Berlin Painter

all that shrieking, gibbering and whistling first thing in the morning is just birds telling one another, 'Keep off, this is my patch'.

It is especially worth climbing one last set of stairs, to Botany, the rest of Zoology and the Aquarium, because here are the live specimens. Do not miss the dead ones first. The section of the Californian redwood tree, which

grew to be over twelve feet in diameter between 550 and 1886 AD, is in Botany. In Entomology are old insect showcases with lids that you lift, one by one, to discover wonderful butterflies, like *Morpho cypris* Westwood, whose delicately-patterned wings suddenly reveal intense violet irridescence as your angle of view moves. Are the leaf forms of the Leaf Insect *Phyllum crurifolium* really animal, not vegetable? Now you can go on to the living specimens. Back in Botany, at the window, is a special bee-hive. In summer, watch the steady stream of returning bees, and try to follow just one as it struggles back through the seething mass. You may see a little space clear around it as it gyrates and wiggles its bottom in the famous dance that tells its colleagues in which direction, and at what distance, it has found a rich supply of pollen.

Finally, at the end of the upper Zoology gallery, there is the aquarium, where you can try to detect a movement in the Spectacled Caiman, or the elegant Long-nosed Treesnake, a lustrous thread of vivid green. My favourites were the terrapins. One of them, the common musk turtle, seemed to wear a permanent, aimiable smile. Looks can be deceptive. He cruised around, intermittently terrorising just one of his four companion red-eared terrapins, elegant chaps with pin-striped faces and necks, just like old-world stockbrokers. Perhaps the stockbroker, *Chrysemys scripta elegans*, had called the musk turtle common. If he let a flipper flap too near the aimiable smile, a lunge and a sharp snap sent him on his way, with a mournful and persecuted look.

Manchester United Museum and Visitor Centre

Manchester United Football Club, Old Trafford, Manchester M16 0RA
(061) 872 1661
Closed Saturdays. 🎟️ 🅿️
▣ (lunchtimes) ♿ W
🚻 & 👫 must book; evening tours sometimes possible in summer; also sometimes possible for tours to visit players' tunnel and dressing rooms – write for details.

Manchester United's museum was opened in 1986, in a bit of spare space above the Club's Matt Busby Suite. It uses trophies, pictures and some cherished relics to present its story in a lively way, to the accompaniment of the sounds of cheering fans. There is plenty of information for visitors with time to pause, cartoon-style summaries of the story for anyone, and lots of videos of great moments in the life of the club, on and off the pitch.

Pictures and documents record a quiet and rather wordy start as the 'Newton Heath (Lancashire and Yorkshire Railway) Cricket and Football Club', established, around 1878, by the Dining Room Committee of the Yorks. and Lancs. Railway Carriage and Waggon Works. Football was just getting going, against a bit of competition, with the development of the Football Alliance, which became the Football League. The club did not do so badly, despite a pitch that was more like a mud-bath, and a half-mile treck to changing accommodation kindly provided in the Three Crowns. They dropped all but the Newton Heath bit of the name, and were known as the Heathens, before acquiring their Manchester name in a reorganisation in the first years of the present century. The reorganisation followed a bit of financial stickiness, and in the process of struggling free, roles became established that have been filled repeatedly with different actors in the dramas of many clubs since. Then as now, players

Live red-eared Terrapin in the Manchester Museum aquarium

Bronze bust of Sir Matt Busby

was ahead of his time. The later displays chronicle the growing commercial importance of football kit, increasing hugely in the 1970s.

Surely the best known of all managers was Sir Matt Busby, and the displays explain why. Appointed in 1945, he detected that some of the players who had returned to football from the War were not as young as they had been when they left, and cannily began in the early 1950s to scour the country for schoolboy talent. At a critical moment in the mid '50s, he courageously replaced several of his veterans with some of his young discoveries, and guided the team into the victorious phase that was tragically interrupted by the air crash in Munich, on February 5th 1958, when eight players and three club officials were amongst the dead. Newspapers of the time and other relics record the shock of the event. There is a telegram, sent before the accident by Duncan Edwards, letting his landlady know that the flight was expected to be cancelled. There is an illuminated testimonial, sent after the event, from the occupants of 'H' Wing at Pentonville. Busby, severely injured, survived, and Manchester United crowned their ten year recovery with the European Cup in 1968.

There are plenty of reminders of other great figures as well. A case is devoted to Bobby Charlton, crammed with the tasseled caps associated with international match victories under his captaincy, and trophies and testimonials of all kinds. There are the football boots of Mark Jones, who died at Munich, and of Norman Whiteside.

1966 World Cup cap

were only part of the story, and the new Manchester United acquired a Manager, Louis Rocca, and a patron, Brewer Davies, won over by the dog that the Club used as a collecting gimmick.

Of course, they did also soon acquire their first mega-star of the pitch, the Welsh Wizard, Billy Meredith. He was not just a pretty pair of feet either, but a founder of the Footballers' Union, and of commercial involvement in the game as well, to judge by the mementoes in the display. We see him

endorsing the benefits of Oxo: 'I am very pleased to say that I consider Oxo an excellent beverage for anyone engaged in athletics, as it gives energy and staying power.' He also seems to have been one of three partners who marketed a football under his name. At least the shirt he wore for the victory over Bristol City in the 1909 FA Cup match at Crystal Palace was not used to advertise washing powder. It is still here, stains and all, for us to see later on in the displays. Perhaps Meredith

Memorabilia of national & international fixtures

Photograph of Billy Meredith, the Welsh Wizard

is all brought to life by the accompanying videos, recording not only great goals on the pitch, but some of the Club's own goals off it as well. One was the parting of the ways with Tommy Docherty, who marked the occasion with the immortal observation 'when one door closes, another slams in your face'.

For the visitor with a less developed interest in the game, perhaps accompanying an enthusiast, the trophies and presentation gifts offer a special study, ranging from huge articles of silver, of which there are splendid arrays, to Wedgwood. The connoisseur will, however, concentrate on the trophies associated with the European Cup, to pick out national characteristics in the elegant lines of an Italian cup, filigree work in a galleon from Portugal, and socialist realism from behind the Iron Curtain. Joint first prize for imagination goes to the Poles, with a presentation vase of 1968, carved from a single piece of coal and achieving a cunning contrast of surface texture in the material, and to the Hungarians for the traditional colt-skin water-carrier, presented in 1984 by Raba Vasas Eto Gyor.

The left hand boot of the latter pair, with, as the label points out, Whiteside's foot inside it, scored the winning goal in the 1985 Cup Final. Nearby is the ball from the 1948 Cup Final Match, and another one with which George Best scored six goals against Northampton Town in 1970. It

The Whitworth Art Gallery

Oxford Road, Manchester M15 6ER
(061) 273 4865
Closed Sundays, but open till
9pm on Thursdays. 🄵 🄳 🄿
♿ W: access to all parts except one
small area.
♨ & ♐ phone to advise of visit,
and for details of services. ◎

The Whitworth Art Gallery displays its collections in a spacious and relaxed style all its own. For many decades, its galleries were just what one might expect from its rather institutional Edwardian exterior, vast, with plaster-casts of classical sculpture marching round the dimly-visible upper reaches of walls, crammed with row upon row of pictures. A radical remodelling in the 1960s lowered ceilings where height was not needed, fitted in new levels instead, and opened up all the spaces into one another in a flowing open plan. The decor has not changed much since, and offers one of the best museum interiors of the period, from a design point of view, to be seen anywhere.

It houses the best collections of En-glish watercolours, of European prints and drawings, and of textiles in the north of England, besides an outstanding selection of English 20th century painting and sculpture, and an extensive and unique archive of wallpaper and its history. Almost all the objects in these collections deteriorate in a very few years with constant exposure to even low levels of light, so that displays are frequently changed. A description of what is on show at any one time only gives an idea of the kind of selection visitors are likely to see from the gallery's huge holdings. There are also a number of major temporary exhibitions of loan material each year, generally on themes related to the specialities of the permanent collections.

The entrance hall gives onto a gallery of textiles. The light level here has to be low, but the textiles, European and Asian, are exotic. Richly coloured fabrics covered in glinting metal-thread embroidery glow within the spacious cases. Some of the most lavish on display when I visited were Chinese imperial robes, decorated with the dragon designs that only the Royal Household was entitled to wear. In central Asia, more subtly decorated fabrics had great value in many societies, especially those whose nomadic ways of life restricted the accumulation of less portable goods. Peoples of the central Asian towns could sometimes identify the home-town and status of a stranger from the patterns of costumes like the exhibited silk velvet ikat coat. Fittings from a Turkman tent were on show, with photographs to explain the traditional arrangements of the tent interior. The richest European embroideries are ecclesiastical, and two German altar-frontals were on display. On the 15th century one, the Tree of Jesse predicted by Isaiah, laden with his descendants, emerged from Jesse's stomach. The 18th century one was notable for the invention that went into the textures of the gold thread-work. In some parts, threads seemed to flow like turbulent water, whilst in others they were lined up in a paving of tiny rectangles. The scrolling shapes they composed, which constantly changed direction just at the point of tightest curvature, were in the style called Rococo. In contrast, among the exceptional tapestries in the collection, is one designed by Eduardo Paolozzi (colour plate 14). Mickey Mouse and Donald Duck are embedded in other brilliantly-coloured motifs derived from the everyday commercial and popular designs that have always fascinated this artist.

There are many themes a visitor

William Blake, The Descent of Peace, *illustrating Milton's 'Hymn on the morning of Christ's Nativity'*

Antonio Pallaiuolo, Battle of the Nude Men, *Renaissance engraving*

'Daisy' wallpaper by William Morris

could follow through whilst looking at the gallery's pictures and sculptures. One might be the contrast between styles of painting that show off the way paint has been applied, preserving individual characteristics, and methods that give a more impersonal effect. Watercolour becomes rather a mess if it is much disturbed once put on, and therefore tends to preserve the hand movements of the watercolourist as faithfully as handwriting. Watercolours tend to be as recognisable as letters from your relatives, and this is a collection in which you can get to know the handwritings. The curves and sharp points of William Blake's figures give them the look of italic script. The English romantic landscapist, Thomas Girtin, built up the textures of ancient masonry in a carpet of little dots, which makes gothic architecture look as if it has been knitted like an Aran sweater. Turner scrawled foliage in characteristic shapes throughout his career, though embedded in an ever-growing repertoire of marks of all sizes.

Some styles of print-making, such as woodcut and steel engraving, repress that kind of spontaneity. Others, such

as etching, were developed specifically because they encouraged it. No one took greater advantage of its possibilities than the 18th century Italian, Piranesi, especially in his series of views of fantastic prison interiors. 'Prison with Circular Tower' is typical. The tower is in the midst of an endless interior, festooned with strange ropes and pulleys, surrounded by staircases and bridges leading nowhere, and sinister openings blocked by massive grilles.

20th century English art strongly contrasts such expressive and individualistic styles with deliberately mechanistic methods. Edward Burra's pictures are even more fantastic than Piranesi's prisons, and instantly recognisable. 'John Deth' is a scene from an Edgar Allen Poe-style party, with death amongst the feathered revellers, in a luridly red-curtained arabesque interior. No artist is more conscious of the feel of his brush on the wood panels he usually uses than Howard

Hodgkin. His 'Interior at Oakwood Court' glows like a fire with a yellow heart. Henry Moore, L.S. Lowry and Francis Bacon are amongst the other artists for whom touch is a vital quality. Further artists, especially of the 1960s and '70s, a period of art in which the collection is unusually strong, wanted to get away from this kind of thing. Richard Hamilton is one who is represented, and the gallery has recently bought two works by Gilbert and George.

Wallpaper might not be expected to be a form of decoration that allowed for much spontaneity, even in the huge hand-painted 18th century panels that are amongst the earliest pieces in the collection. Nonetheless, one of William Morris's earlier designs represented, 'Bower', is patterned with freely-drawn leaves, which are reminiscent of the shapes in Matisse cut-outs, and dotted with brightly-coloured flowers. Even a design like this, in which the repeat of the pattern would be hard to spot, has a

Detail of late 15th century Altar Frontal with the Tree of Jesse, Cologne region of Germany

Jacob Epstein, Genesis, *1931*

OLDHAM

Oldham Art Gallery

Union Street, Oldham OL1 1DN
(061) 678 4651

and

Local Interest Museum

Greaves Street, Oldham
Closed Tuesday afternoons and all day Sunday. ▣
♿ S: access to Art Gallery difficult, but lift being installed 1989; wheelchair access to Local Interest Museum by arrangement only.
🚻 & 🚻 booking essential for Local Interest Museum (where numbers at one time are limited), and desirable for Art Gallery; to book, and for details of facilities, workshops and events, phone Keeper of Social History for the Local Interest Museum, and Exhibitions Outreach Officer for the Art Gallery. ☺

Oldham's Art Gallery and Local Interest Museum are both in different parts of its main library buildings, and both have recently enjoyed an injection of new funds. The Local Interest Museum has just opened a long term exhibition called 'Going up town – shopping in Oldham c. 1920', which includes a reconstruction of a short street of shops. The Art Gallery is renovating its good collection of English watercolours, which includes several Turners. Some of the oil paintings have recently been restored, too, revealing in the process the stunning primary colour scheme of 'Balshazzer's Feast' of 1836, by the rare visionary painter, Samuel Colman. It has interesting later 19th and 20th century English pictures, and a large collection of 1960s and '70s prints. The gallery also collects contemporary photographs, and has been entrusted with looking after the photography collection of the North West Regional Arts Association as well. In 1986, it was

chosen as one of a number of galleries to receive funding from the Arts Council, under a scheme intended to ginger up the presentation of contemporary art. Oldham is dedicating its share towards a programme that aims to involve audiences in the community that have tended to be deterred, even offended, by traditional galleries. There are also plans to extend the exhibition space, and introduce catering.

Art Galleries look peaceful enough, but the art world itself has always been wracked by bitter disputes. If the pictures in most galleries could speak, they would hurl abuse at one another. Plenty of rancour hides behind the good manners on Oldham's walls. Just about everything in the collection would gang up against the biggest picture, John Collier's 'Death of Cleopatra'. It presents a scene of some disorder, at the feet of monumental figures of Antony and Cleopatra as gods. Cleopatra has killed herself, her companion Iras sprawls dead at her feet, and another attendant, Charmian, has not got long to go. Technically it is extremely good, which, combined with its jumbo dimensions, has always made it a hit. The gold sheet under Cleopatra is an especially flashy bit of painting. But dramatically, Collier was not up to it. It is banal. If Cleopatra was a little less pale, the ladies might just be recovering from an enviably abandoned lunch. Moreover, it is erotically titillating. A number of academicians of the period were adept at dressing up painting that was really soft porn in impec-

Jeweller at work, reconstructed street

rigorous geometric basis hidden behind it, and in later designs the geometry became much more apparent. Highly stylised designs like 'Acanthus' suited the woodblock printing technique used for most wallpapers, though that design did call for thirty blocks to print the different colours.

Perhaps the greatest master of stylised turn-of-the-century wallpaper design was Walter Crane. His wallpapers in the collection display a unique marriage of awful lumpy figure drawing with a truly wonderful sense of pattern. One of his tricks is to make the central figures in a design low in contrast, so that they are dominated by high contrast, heavily-outlined spaces between them, an effect that is strangely decorative. The designer Voysey was a master of this kind of trick, too. Some of his furniture is on show as well, and he continued to design into the 1930s. The wallpaper archive includes a mass of more recent design, and is a resource for artists, or just for anyone wondering whether to paper the room this time, instead of painting it, and seeking inspiration.

cable artistic credentials. The credentials humbugged galleries like Oldham, which bought the pictures, whilst the titillation, as a leaflet accompanying the painting explains, attracted bizarre tinkering, by restorers as well as vandals.

Many painters of the period travelled miles to get away from that kind of dishonesty. Specifically, the thing was to board and lodge in a remote and deprived fishing or rural community, and paint Life in the Raw. Oldham has quite a lot of this kind of thing. Stanhope Forbes was very good at it, and there is a scene by him of a countryman's horse pausing to drink. Painters sympathetic to this approach also flirted with new ways of painting. The high horizon and rectangular forms of Edward Stott's painting, 'The Ferry', suggest that he had been looking at Japanese pictures. Edward Hornel certainly had. By this stage in his life he was turning out pictures all of a pattern, little girls with soft round faces in landscapes that seem to glitter, because of the sharp edges to the slabs of cool bright paint, applied with a palette knife. Many of Oldham's paintings of this period show experiments with bold paint and colour of this kind.

The mutual hostility between these painters and older academicians was sweetness and light compared with the battles that followed over 20th century art. Oldham has good examples by many figures now revered, who faced an uphill struggle in their day. There are beautiful landscapes by Paul Nash and Graham Sutherland, an Alan Davie abstract, and more recent works by Tom Phillips and David Hockney. But all these figures are now associated with an art market that many younger artists feel has either sold out to, or been hijacked by, a small, privileged establishment. It is an audience, some feel, that brandishes art as a weapon of social one-upmanship – with emphasis on the 'man', in the eyes of many women in the art world. Oldham is determined not to get trapped in this kind of thing, so only a little of its permanent collection is on show at a time. Much of the gallery space is left as a platform for new voices. It pro-

Part of the reconstructed shopping street of about 1920

J. M. W. Turner, Bellinzona – The Bridge over the Ticino, *watercolour*

vides an opportunity for everyone to discover their own position on these issues.

The theatrically presented street scene in the basement of the Local Interest Museum, round the corner from the Art Gallery, provides a setting for real rescued fittings from commercial premises. The dates vary, but nothing is later than the 1930s, and the overall effect is earlier. The detailing is based on painstaking research. In the pawnbrokers, only the unredeemed pledges are displayed. The others are discreetly wrapped, lest the recognition of some pledged item betray a secret embarrassment to friends or relatives. The parcels, labelled and waiting patiently in rows on the shelves, are of brown paper crumpled with frequent re-use. Perhaps the cash that should redeem them is disappearing in the Crown and Mitre across the road, with its pigeon-fanciers' certificates, and stuffed prize fish. Nearby is a view of spinning mules, through a workshop window.

A particularly successful feature of Oldham's version of this idea are the figures in costume. These are always difficult for museums, and are often hilariously inappropriate (like a 1950s shop dummy, with long curling fingers and glamour eye-lashes, standing outside a desert tent in a recent touring display about the Bedouin). Oldham, I feel, has hit just the right note, not too life-like, but with lots of characterisation. The pharmacist, with his bow tie and greying hair, would clearly see himself a cut above the taxidermist – an Oldham speciality – trying to put life back into very dead specimens in his dingy workshop. The young watchmender, absorbed in a problem at his window, exudes professional confidence to fit his particularly handsome jeweller's premises. His shop benefits from a grand window of stained glass, celebrating the Modern Age, with a central figure holding dividers and a cog-wheel, against a background including a telescope and a steam engine; surrounding her are lunettes of the thinkers that someone reckoned carried the torch of advanced thinking in their day, including Erasmus, Herzog and Donatello.

The shopping theme continues in some of the displays upstairs, with a video film and stills of the real thing in Oldham, and also space for temporary installations on other themes.

PADIHAM

Gawthorpe Hall

Padiham, Nr Burnley, Lancashire
BB12 8UA   (0282) 78511
Open Good Friday/beginning of April (whichever is earlier) to October, but closed all day Mondays, Fridays, and all other mornings. 🕎 ▣ 🅿
 ST: wheelchair access to ground floor only.
🚻 & 🍴 phone Warden to book, and for details of extensive programme of activities. ◎

Gawthorpe, one of only two historic houses owned by the National Trust in Lancashire, would be a spectacular Jacobean mansion to visit even if empty. As it is, thanks to the life work of Rachel Kay-Shuttleworth, who grew up here, this is the place to find one of the very finest collections of needlework in the country. She devoted her life to needlework and to public service, and in 1953 was offered the chance to combine the two at Gawthorpe, at the age of 67. Her interest in needlework was not just aesthetic. She

saw it as a way of bringing the training of hand together with eye and mind back into higher education, an ideal of the arts and crafts movement, prominent when she was growing up, deeply unfashionable in the 1950s, but now again attracting more attention. She worked to establish Gawthorpe as a centre for the crafts, raising considerable sums of money through a foundation, and negotiating with the National Trust. She saved the house from dereliction by running around with buckets and clearing snow from the roof, though in her seventies. So it was due to her that Gawthorpe was put on a reliable footing. Now house and collection are cared for, but visitors who see only the static displays miss the archive of needlework here, and the extensive programme of activities associated with it.

The interior is as splendid as the exterior, though much of it is not as old as it might look. Bits of it have been extensively remodelled with features in the Victorian imitation-Jacobean style, more Jacobean than the Jacobeans, especially by Pugin and Barry. The richest room is the drawing room, the last room visited on the ground floor. Its wonderful plaster ceiling and frieze really are Jacobean, five months' work at sixpence a day in 1605 for plasterers

Exterior view of Gawthorpe Hall

The Drawing Room, showing original panelling & ceiling, with mid-19th century furniture

Detail of a walnut chair in the Queen Anne style, with marquetry decoration

Francis and Thomas Gunby. Armoured knights, ladies, gentlemen and griffins guard the corners and windows, spiralling vines and grapes, looking a bit like strawberries, coil across the ceiling. The panelling, with inlaid designs, is of the same period, in the Italian style then quite newly fashionable. The furniture is very fine, too, but of later date. The set of walnut chairs, with curved backs inlaid with birds and flowers, and accompanying table on a bulging hexagonal pillar, are Queen Anne. The massive gothic-style oak and walnut inlay table in the middle of the room is by Pugin and Crace, and the olde-world oak armchairs of strange elephant-ear shape, which try hard to go with the panelling, are also Victorian revivals.

There are more particularly curious rooms at the very top of the Victorian staircase. The first is the Long Gallery, fulfilling its original function as a picture and promenading gallery, and with original ceiling plaster. The fire grate, though, is by Pugin, and the startling wallpaper is a recent reprint. Another remarkable reprint paper has recently been put in the other room also at this level, the Huntroyde bedroom, though this time it is a gentle design, by Walter Crane. In this room the show is stolen by the bed. If ever there was a bed to sit up in and see a ghost, this is it. A four poster affair of the early 19th century, it seems assembled from ancient bits and pieces. The jet-black oak bedhead, which rears up behind the sleeper (should he or she be rash enough to drop off), is coffered, with strange carved figures and inlays, and the canopy looms overhead on bulging crenellated columns. Rachel Kay-Shuttleworth did nothing to lighten the effect by devoting the spare hours of ten years of her early life to embroidering for it, in Jacobean-style crewel-work, the most magnificent hangings and counterpane.

The heart of the house is in the series of bedrooms at first and second floor level, newly fitted with special cases of the display of some 500 specimens of needlework at a time from the 15,000 in the collection. Lighting levels are low, to preserve the colour

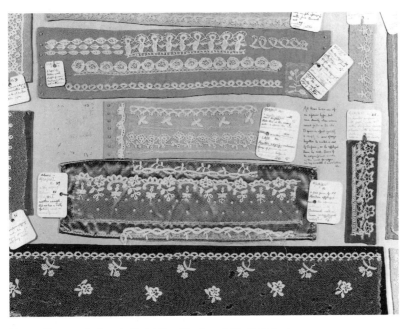

A page of lace samples from the Rachel Kay-Shuttleworth Textile Collections

PORT SUNLIGHT

Lady Lever Art Gallery

Port Sunlight Village, Bebington,
Wirral L62 5EQ
(051) 645 3623
Open daily. Unaccompanied
children under 16 not admitted.

V **▣** **P** **&**

♿ & **♟** for bookings and
information about services, phone
the Gallery, or the Education
Officer at the Walker Art Gallery,
Liverpool (051 207 0001).

The Lady Lever Gallery is a gallery
that has to be seen in its setting to be
understood. It was opened by the first
Lord Leverhulme in 1922, after thirty-
five years or so of making a fortune out
of Sunlight Soap, and commemorates
his wife. It is situated in the heart of the
'village', a group of some 900 houses
designed by a variety of architects, and
offering every variation of the high-
gabled, giant-cottage style of domestic
architecture introduced by Lutyens
and Norman Shaw, with plenty of trees
and a fountain. Leverhulme, who had
started life as William Lever of Bolton,
was determined to provide surroundings for his employees that would allow
healthy development of mind as well as
body, with amenities such as front and
back gardens for all. His creation was
not the only such Utopian development, but is surely the best preserved.
His brand of patrician social control is
no longer the flavour of the month, but
it served to set useful standards. His
gallery, a memorial to his wife, was a
way of employing in the same cause the
art collection that had been one of his
passions.

The heart of the building is a large
main gallery, with smaller rooms and a
rotunda at each end, a row of galleries
running down each side, and two small
balcony galleries at first-floor level. It
is a treasure house of ceramics, furniture, and tapestry, but is most renowned for its Victorian paintings.
They are the very best of their kind,
and again and again the visitor with a

and fabric of the threads, and displays
will be changed quite frequently, for
the same reason. Only a little searching
is needed to discover traces of Rachel
Kay-Shuttleworth's assiduous cura-
torship. One of her labels is attached to
a Kashmiri shawl, meticulously recording its source, condition, repairs carried out, and comments on articles of
its kind. There are more little labels on
the page displayed from the folder of
lace specimens that she kept for
teaching: 'a complex design of dainty
effect, with trolly used on one edge',
and 'an effective lace, but very likely to
"scrumple" as it is so open.' The
museum has admirably carried on this
tradition, with panels on which the
technicalities of this particular world
are explained, accompanied by excellent diagrams of many stitches. Picot,
couching, cross-stitch, chenille,
stroked gathers, hollie point and
dozens of other handy terms will arm
anyone with some attentiveness to
spare with mastery of an impressive
new set of jargon. Others may prefer
just to gaze, expertly or not, on everything from embroidered waistcoats and

Drawing Room ceiling detail, 1600–05

household linen of the 18th century to
patchwork quilts of the 20th.

All around the house, visitors may
notice unusually interesting portraits,
roughly contemporary with the style of
the house, including Purcell, Pepys,
John Locke and Charles II. There are
some thirty in all, from the reserves of
the National Portrait Gallery, London.
Gawthorpe is one of only four houses
around Britain with a substantial loan.

John Everett Millais, A Dream of the Past: Sir Isumbras at the Ford, *1857*

English 'Bull' commode, c.1770

prior enthusiasm in the field experiences a momentary delight on finding that this is the home of yet another much-reproduced example. Amongst the big names, there is Holman Hunt's 'May Morning on Magdalen Tower', Millais' 'Sir Isumbras', Lord Leighton's 'Garden of the Hesperides', and Maddox Brown's 'Cromwell on his Farm'. But it is perhaps the outstandingly good works by lesser known figures that come as the greatest surprise. In Herkomer's 'Last Muster', as the Chelsea Pensioners sing in chapel, one old trooper turns anxiously to touch the sleeve of his quiet neighbour, his face betraying dawning realisation that it is too late to call the doctor. There is one of the very best of Joseph Farquharson's winter scenes, looking into the sun through branches, which cast a tracery of shadows on the snow, with the usual cast of amiably woolly sheep. And there is Edward Gregory's 'Boulter's Lock', along with two oil sketches, which give us a little insight into the processes of working out the composition.

Up on the north balcony is a special treat, a selection of the paintings that Lever bought because, in the days before copyright protection for artists, once he had bought them he could adapt them to advertise soap. J. Esley's 'The Wash Tub' is a particular treasure, presenting a super-granny, eighty if she is a day, with suitably frilly cap. She is possessed of demonic health and good humour, taking a muscular swipe with soapy cloth at one of the three children who, together with their dog, are reducing wash-day to a foam and shriek-filled shambles. Not all artists appreciated finding their work used for commerce. W.P. Frith was happy enough to sell to Lever in 1889 his painting 'The New Frock', a winsome illustration of childish vanity, showing a little girl raising her smock to show off her acquisition; but he was outraged to come across a reproduction of it with the slogans 'Sunlight Soap', and 'So Clean', written across it. Lever clearly relished the furious public squabble that followed, and betrayed no hint of doubt about his right to use artistic productions in this way.

Wedgwood ewer, green jasper with lilac reliefs

Instead he complained how hard it was to find suitable paintings, and gleefully described proposed adaptations of ones he did find, such as replacing the glass in the hand of the best man toasting a bride with a bar of soap.

The rotundas at each end of the building are full of sculpture, mostly late nineteenth century at the entrance end and ancient classical works at the far end. The other smaller galleries offer special treasures worth seeking out for almost every taste. There is an outstanding collection of Wedgwood. The Chinese ceramics are mostly 18th century, but with an early copy of a 9th century set of miniature processional grave figures, a sort of poor man's 'Emperor's Warriors'. The furniture is magnificent. Amongst many star pieces, note a flamboyant mid-18th century cabinet, encrusted with gilded decoration on every edge. It was designed to show off small panels representing Orpheus and wild animals, made of the thinnest slices of coloured marbles and stones. It is shown in the William and Mary room, and there are a number of other period room set-

tings. One room is pastiche, designed for Leverhulme in the Adam manner by the 1920s designer Percy McQuoid. Others have the advantage of authentic panelling from demolished houses.

The collection is especially rich in good examples of things that are often seen only in faded condition. In one room are watercolours, including wonderful ones by Turner. They are displayed in a set of hinged frames, which can be browsed through like the leaves of a book. Shown in rotation, they include a fine early view of Wells Cathedral and outstanding later scenes, with a brilliantly sunny 'Bolton Abbey' and a spectacularly gloomy 'Dudley Castle', all clouds and smoke and flame. The vivid colours that have survived so well in these examples have survived less well in the tapestries, but an exception to this is 'Hero and Leander', with rich blues and reds, from England's main 17th century centre of production at Mortlake. There is a delightful collection of smaller embroideries and stumpwork of the period too, displayed in rotation. Notice the 'Drowning of Pharoah in the Red Sea', watched by Moses, Aaron and the Israelites, a splendid confusion of arms and spears and faces suspended in the water, with an improbable Pharoah, and even a mermaid. Other specimens seem to bear out a point made about these embroideries by recent women historians: the women who made the embroideries often sought out for their subjects biblical stories showing women in positive roles, rarely chosen by male artists and patrons.

Briton Riviere, Fidelity, *1869*

PRESCOT

Prescot Museum

34 Church Street, Prescot, Merseyside
L34 3LA   (051) 430 7787
Closed Mondays. ▣
&️ S: wheelchair access very limited.
♦ & ♦ should book in advance: phone Curator to book and for information about services; refreshments may be available for pre-booked parties by arrangement.

Prescot Museum offers a small but modern and informative display on the history of clock and watchmaking, a local speciality from 1600. The fine clocks and watches in the collection can be seen in the context of the technical and social background in which they were produced. The displays are all on the first floor of an 18th century house. The ground floor is used for a programme of temporary exhibitions on natural history and scientific subjects, as well as of work by local artists and craftspeople.

The display begins with a survey of time-keeping devices, and the innovations on which improvements in accuracy and convenience depended. There is a sundial, which involved quite tricky geometry, and a nocturnal, little more than an engraved disc of brass with a swivelling pointer, for sighting on the stars. This one is a small, handy 18th century version, but the idea derives from the astrolabes of antiquity. Early spring-driven portable clocks and watches were twice as accurate, but a bit bulky. A mid-16th century one here is a cylindrical box, two inches high and three deep, a bit large for the pocket. The size soon came down, and the earliest local watch (1607) by Thomas Aspinwall of Toxteth is almost handy. One of the secrets of all these early devices was the 'fusee', an ingenious device to compensate for the weakening of the spring as it unwinds; it is almost the shape of a mole's nose, a tapering cone about which a delicate chain spirals. Much better timekeeping came with the pendulum, applied to clocks by Christian Huyghens in 1656, and with balances in watches. Many refinements followed, as the display explains.

Watch-making in Prescot was a business distributed in hundreds of small workshops, in the attics of individual homes. Only a few men became established as makers, commissioning the parts from numerous workshops, assembling them, and supplying under their own names the completed watches and clocks that we see in these displays. Most workers specialised in turning out just a few parts. Pinions or studs, pillars or springs, there were dozens to chose from. There are reconstructions of specialised benches for a number of processes. One of the attic shops was still in use in the 1950s, so we can see a photograph of it – long, rather basic, a bit dingy. In such places boys from twelve years old or so would pass a seven-year apprenticeship, well placed from a health point of view compared with their contemporaries in the mines or mills. The certificate binding Michael Beesley as an apprentice, 'aged thirteen years or thereabouts' in 1797, is on display. Michael is described as a poor boy, his certificate signed by the churchwarden and the overseers of the poor. His father had been a shoemaker, but Michael stood to improve himself in his trade. He was bound to a maker not of parts, but of the precision tools needed to make them, an expertise of higher skill and status. Michael had, according to the standard form of such agreements, to avoid fornicating and frequenting taverns or evil company. His master, by a handwritten codicil to the document, undertook to fit him out with a decent new suit, at the end of the seven years.

The Swiss only got in on the act towards the end of the last century, but came in with a vengeance when they did. It was obvious that the workshop system could not compete, and a Prescot man was dispatched to America, to study factory methods. On his return, in a bold initiative chronicled here, they set up in the last decade of the 19th century a spanking new works,

Wheel-cutting engine by Wyke and Green, c.1780

with all modern conveniences and a few hours' education a week for younger workers. No married women were allowed as workers, though. The powers that be, men to a man, thought that married women should be at home, 'looking after the comforts of family life'. The bold enterprise could turn out 1,200 identical watches in one run, and brimming boxes of hundreds of components remain to bear witness to the scale of production. The machines that made it possible are also here, such as the automatic wig-wag pinion polishing machine, which kept count of the number of automatic strokes of its buffer, so that it knew when to stop and set to work on the next pinion. You can compare it, proudly harnessed up with a leather belt to the overhead power shaft in a reconstruction of the new work-bench, with its humble hand-operated ancestor on the work-bench displayed next door. Unfortunately, the

management was out-marketed by the super-efficient Swiss and Americans, and the enterprise failed in 1911. Sad receipts on show record the sale of furniture and machinery in small lots. The building was used within a few years as a barracks for the Accrington Pals, off to the trenches from which so few returned.

The Swiss industry really took off with the triumph of the wristwatch, whose history is presented here. Perhaps it was one of those ideas no one quite believed could ever prove popular. The earliest example on show, an Ingersoll of 1914, looks like a half-hearted try-on. It is really just a pocket-watch, not such a small one either, cobbled onto a huge strap, more like a weapon than a wristwatch. Demand soon led to miniaturisation, and to special features. One group of users with a more than usually pressing interest in keeping an eye on the time,

The sundial, Prescot Museum

A box of flywheels used in watchmaking

PRESTON

Harris Museum and Art Gallery

Market Square, Preston, Lancashire PR1 2PP   (0772) 58248
Closed Sundays. 🄵 ◼
♿ W: ramped entrance, lift to main galleries, stair lift to mezzanine levels.
🚹 & 🚻 phone Education Officer to give notice, to book guided visits (which may sometimes be arranged to take place out-of-hours), and for information about other extensive services and activities. ☺

When you are warned that a museum you are to visit is above the library, magnificence is generally the last thing you expect. The Harris Museum is an exception, installed above the library in a huge neoclassical building, which is splendid inside and out, and truly a fine structure, not just municipal pomp. Until recently, the effect was spoiled by a confusing entrance, but a new and welcoming entrance area has now been constructed, which includes an installation commissioned from sculptor Ian Hamilton Finlay. The large galleries are arranged around a great square hall, the full height of the building, with a circular balcony at first-floor level, and a square one at second-floor level. A small balcony, high up under the ceiling, gives access (for pre-booked groups only) to close examination of paintings of Egypt by John Somerscales, whilst at lower levels are no less than three tiers of casts of Greek sculpture.

We reach the two main balconies and their adjoining galleries via another hall running the full height of the building, containing a grand staircase, hung with large Victorian and Edwardian paintings. The museum has good local history displays, and exceptional collections of English paintings and decorative art. Its gallery of costume has recently been remodelled, and a new gallery created for prints,

but rather tricky requirements, were deep-sea divers. Rolex came up with a tough, waterproof answer by 1940. It was self-winding too, in case they forgot to wind it; awful to have to try and wind a watch with those big gloves on, 200 fathoms down. But the Swiss finally got caught out in their turn, by the quartz crystal and digital watches of the Japanese. The tiny, delicate sprays of evenly-spaced golden connections in the integrated circuits, revealed for us to inspect in this display, even look a bit like the rising sun of the Japanese flag.

Arthur Devis, Portrait of John Orlebar of Hinwick House, Bedfordshire, *c.1740*

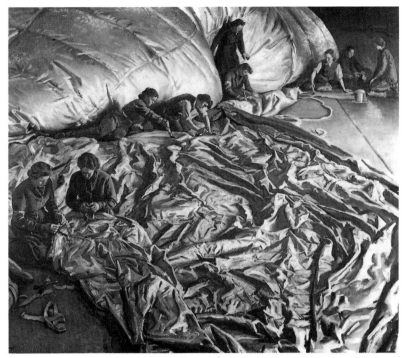

Dame Laura Knight, In for Repairs

Underwear of the 1860s, with crinoline

watercolours and drawings. The Harris is also one of a dozen or so regional galleries around the country to have benefitted in recent years from a decision by the Arts Council to make funds available for the promotion of contemporary art in local authority galleries like this one. Preston uses its allocation for an exhibition programme that includes innovative, and perhaps provocative, new work, as well as shows with popular appeal. The wide range of temporary exhibitions is accompanied by a full programme of workshops and activities for the public. The museum has also built up a collection of work by contemporary artists.

The walls of the lower balcony are lined with cases containing a very fine collection of ceramics and glass, especially of Staffordshire, London and Derby wares. The English ceramic industry always suffered from a tendency to feel inferior as regards taste. At its best, its products have a slightly folksy air, offering wares reflecting, for better or worse, traditional culture. Decoration could be an inventive use of the possibilities of the clay, like the delicate relief tracery on some pale cream earthenwares here, or the cheerful marblings in the body of Whieldon-type ware. Unfortunately, wares from overseas seemed, as the 18th century drew onwards, to demonstrate superior taste, which many sectors of the industry felt obliged to imitate for the end of the market that considered itself discerning. Wedgwood, Derby and Worcester in particular turned out volumes of ceramics imitating the forms of antique decoration, oriental porcelain, or German figure-work, but arguably without the wonderful qualities of the originals. Now, not everyone would agree with that, but decide for yourself, with the help of these excellent collections. At least the set of chessmen by John Flaxman, who did many designs for Wedgwood, are lively. But why are the white King and Queen so much more aggressive than the blue? There is also good glassware on this balcony.

Escape into the Story of Preston, in the galleries off the balcony. The first surviving marks of man here are the injuries made by his weapons in the bones of the unfortunate Poulton Elk. Some of the wounds had time to heal in a chase that lasted two or three weeks. An elk was a resource of food and materials worth the investment of that much time and more for a hunting group, and this one survived seventeen wounds before it finally escaped, only by falling beyond the reach of pursuers, through the ice of a pond. There in the mud its bones survived, witnesses to an episode in a harsh era that ended badly for everyone. 8,000 years on, what strange incident resulted in the accumulation of skulls, animal remains and a boat, found when Preston Dock was excavated a century ago? A mere 3,000 years later, the inventor and industrialist, Richard Arkwright, born in Preston in 1732, pursued his goals with relentless success, though he started life as a barber and wigmaker. Amongst his innovations was the water-frame, for spinning several threads of cotton at once. A huge model of Horrockses mill in 1912 testifies to Preston's importance as a cotton town.

A wonderful portrait painter of the 18th century, Arthur Devis, came from Preston, and the display includes some of the portraits commissioned from him by local pillars of the community; others by him are in the galleries upstairs. His pictures of doll-like figures in sparsely-furnished interiors or simple landscapes look charming and quaint now, but their lack of fussiness was actually the last word in down-to-earth modernity in its day. One picture here intrigued me, the portrait of 'Francis Vincent, his wife Mercy, and daughter Ann, of Weddington Hall, Warwickshire, set in a misty grey landscape. What is the piece of paper with which Francis Vincent sternly approaches his fashionably-dressed wife? From the look on his face, this might be a bill, and mercy not her name but what he expects her to ask for. (The true meaning of the paper, and of the picture's narrative, is now lost: Francis Vincent was a Barrister-at-Law of the Inner Temple, and must have commissioned this painting to record the receipt of an important

document, whose content and nature are today unknown.)

The top balcony of the main hall contains a wonderful collection, some of Mrs French's bequest of 2,700 scent bottles and 1,000 card cases. They are distinguished by an exuberance of decoration, which often goes over the top, and come in every imaginable variety of shape and size, vividly coloured and textured, with lots of gold (colour plate 3). In one gallery off the balcony are regularly changing displays of costume, dimly lit to preserve the colours and stuff of the fabrics. A new mezzanine gallery shows a programme of various exhibitions of watercolours, prints and drawings.

Cream-coloured earthenware teapot, c.1765–75

The top floor also houses the picture galleries, lofty, newly-painted and brightly lit to leave no trace of the gloom that is sometimes associated with municipal galleries of art. The kind of pictures that are usually found in such galleries are here, but mostly on the staircases and second floor balcony. The displays in the main galleries are often changed, drawing on strong collections of earlier 20th century English painting, including work by Stanley Spencer, and a virtuoso painting of barrage-balloon repairs by Dame Laura Knight. The room of recent purchases offers a chance to see a striking painting by Maggi Hambling, 'July Sunrise, Orwell Estuary 2', and painted landscapes developed from giant photographs by Ian McKeever, as well as work by Michael Sandle and Kate Whiteford.

Lancashire County and Regimental Museum

Stanley Street, Preston, Lancashire PR1 4YP
(0772) 264075
Closed Thursdays and Sundays.
🄵 🄿
♿ : wheelchair access to ground floor only **XT**; rest of museum **S**. 🏨 & 🚻 phone Curator to give notice of large groups and for details of services.

Outside this museum we are greeted by what look like robots from an alien civilisation, giant cast-iron cones bigger than a person, with slits for eyes. They are shelters for air raid wardens from World War Two, and set the military tone for the museum, where the emphasis is on the history of three of the County's regiments, though there are displays of civilian history as well. This is one of seven museums run by the Lancashire County Museum Service, and all the displays are imaginatively and recently installed. The museum opened only in 1986, in the old Assizes buildings. Besides the permanent displays, there is a central area for temporary installations, initially presenting Lancashire in World War Two, and galleries for art exhibitions, where the emphasis of the programme will be contemporary, a showcase for artists working all over Lancashire today. But the space is not exclusively for art shows: on a recent visit, it was crammed with a collection of historic washing machines second to none.

The three regiments are the Queen's Lancashire Regiment, the Duke of Lancaster's Own Yeomanry, and the 14th/20th King's Hussars. The Queen's Lancashire Regiment displays are on two floors at the far end of the museum from the entrance. Downstairs the highlight is a reconstruction of a section of First-World-War trench, with sounds and reminiscences, and an officer's dug-out. Records as well as mementoes fill in the historical detail. On a lectern near the trench reconstruction, we can read

Harry Kingsley, POW Camp, Korea, *1944*

*Uniform of a Lieutenant, 14th Hussars,
c.1910*

World War II air-raid clearance scene

record some of the acts of special heroism on such days. Also here is a reconstruction of another side of regimental life, an officers' mess from the Victorian era, with the table laid for dinner. Notice the gleaming regimental plate, and the dinner gong made from a shell and its charge case.

The Duke of Lancaster's Own Yeomanry had a gallant history, too, beginning as a volunteer regiment at the start of what became the Napoleonic Wars. However, as records here recall, yeomanry are also associated with another great episode in Lancashire history, the Peterloo Massacre. A wave of great economic hardship followed the triumphal end of the Napoleonic Wars in 1815, with disturbances of all kinds. The yeomanry, policing a mass meeting in Manchester in 1819, tried to move into the crowd to make arrests, but with excessive violence because of their inexperience. The regular 15th Hussars had to be sent in to rescue them, and in the ensuing panic eleven people died and 400 were injured.

Back at the entrance end of the museum, on the upper floors, is 'A King's Hussar, Life in the Cavalry, 1715–1938', giving an idea of life in a regular cavalry regiment. The business of getting soldiers to sign up is not fluffed over. 'Those that are acquainted with a military life', it is recalled, 'knows the recruiting parties are not backward with speaking a little untruth at those times'. Amongst the glimpses of reality, not looking too disagreeable at all, is a reconstruction of sleeping quarters in a camp in India in the 1930s.

The museum is also full of details of the less martial side of military life, Major Shaw, in the 1840s, assembled an album of exquisite Indian miniatures of palaces and gateways, with cool, tiled courtyards. There are artefacts by the English soldiers themselves, such as the soldier's bed-kit layout, modelled in gold and silver by Corporal Gray, which won a prize at the Soldier's Industrial Exhibition at Poona in 1884. No approving reward would have been given to Harry Kingsley, had his intense drawings of life in a

the special order of the day for 28th June, 1916, advising the troops, 'You are about to attack the enemy in far greater numbers than he can oppose to you, supported by huge numbers of guns . . .' Then we can read the reports of the resulting catastrophe, met by an enemy who had anticipated the attack by four hours, long enough to prepare a devastating reception. Upstairs, citations with the medals displayed vividly

Mess scene, Queen's Lancs. Regiment

Japanese prisoner-of-war camp in Korea been discovered. His guards would hardly have been flattered by their portraits, and his drawings also recorded the little illicit triumphs of prison life, such as the dangerous smuggling past the camp guards of a piece of firewood.

The informative displays of Lancashire's civilian life include fittings from a court, a prison cell and a classroom. These are not replicas, but real fittings. Try them for size, they are robust enough, and intended literally to give visitors the feel of the past. The wooden bench is much damaged by furious blows, the rusted cell door engraved with the names of tenants. There is a photograph of stocks in use as late as 1865, at Colne, with three 'wrong-doers' watched over by a top-hatted PC. The justices' chairs from the Liverpool Sessions House are altogether more comfortable. There are school desks to try, too, with brass ink-wells. A pile of books gives the flavour of suitable reading of the age, such as *Leila in England* by Ann Fraser Tyller. 'You must prepare yourself', Leila's Father is saying at one telling point, 'to meet with many little girls who will be both cross and rude to you.' 'Oh, no, Papa', says Leila, 'I am sure they will not be ...' For something more manly, try the pictures of lumberjacks in 'the British Dominions'. The display comes more up-to-date as well. Here is a photograph of stern men in raincoats and trilby hats, surely gumshoes of the Bogart era in action. But no, they are only weights and measures inspectors, checking out a Preston grocer's in the 1950s.

RUNCORN

Norton Priory Museum

Warrington Road, Runcorn, Cheshire WA7 1RE   (0928) 569895
Closed daily till noon; walled garden open March to October.

W: access good to all parts of museum, but not all of site; G in walled garden only.

& must book in advance; phone for details of an extensive choice of tours available for both school and adult groups, and to request a booking form; sessions can be arranged for morning and evening visits.

Norton Priory Museum is one of those sites that offer a wealth of clues to the hidden history of England. The clues were literally hidden until recently. Most of the site had been a wilderness since 1928, when a Georgian house

Figure of St Christopher

was demolished, leaving only some medieval buildings. In 1970 plans were made to begin what became the largest excavation to date, to modern scientific standards, of an English monastic site.

Norman doorway in the undercroft

Now the results allow us to piece together centuries of change here and bring to life some of the great themes of English history. For 400 years, from early in the 12th century, we can follow the fortunes of the small religious foundation of a Norman baron, which became a great monastic institution, only to meet the sudden end that befell all such institutions in England when the exasperated Henry VIII suppressed them in 1536. Then, for another 400 years, we can see the growing wealth and power of one of the great landed families, whose rising fortunes were first demonstrated by the construction of a tudor mansion on the site of the suppressed monastery, incorporating many of the outer monastery buildings. The descendants of the family who built that house replaced it with a Georgian house in 1730, remodelled later in the century by the celebrated architect James Wyatt. It came to a sad end, by demolition, in the 1920s, when the costs of its upkeep became impractical.

We follow the story through displays of artefacts in a modern building, which leads on to the remaining original medieval undercroft, and a viewing gallery for the excavations. An audiovisual presentation near the entrance to the main exhibition space gives a summary of the history of the site. Around the room are displays on the benefactors of the religious foundation, and about daily life within it. A large model shows the monastic buildings, and there are artefacts from all phases of the history of the site. The model presents the buildings as they were in the 15th century. The multitude of finds when the site was excavated illuminate intriguing details, but as always raise problems as well. Why did a number of the skulls found buried here have the harmless but unusual bulge at the back that we can see? It is suggested that some odd practice of swaddling in infancy may be the cause. Other remains reveal the usual sad evidence of lives blighted by chronic disease. A more cheerful feature of the site was especially fine tile work, and the excavations revealed the kiln in which the craftsmen fired the tiles, and many details of their working practice.

General view of the excavations from the observation room

A Tudor shoe

The excavators also managed to save for display in the museum the largest remaining specimen of mosaic tiling in the country, dating from the 14th century (colour plate 4). The later history of the houses is presented with pictures, ceramics and a tudor shoe, and a large manuscript 18th century map of the estate and neighbourhood. Photographs record an Edwardian swansong, of overfurnished rooms and celebrations in marquees.

Outside are the remaining medieval buildings. A real architectural treasure has been lost to us, if the surviving doorway of 1180 is a reliable indication. It is the finest in the county. Nearby, at the end of a passage where visitors to the Priory would probably have waited, is another rare treasure, an eleven-foot-high 14th century statue of St. Christopher, crossing the river with the infant Christ on his shoulders. Like the doorways, it bears witness to the rich art of the past, of which we have little record today. It is unusually lively, with fishes swimming around the saint's feet.

Upstairs is a comfortable viewing gallery, with a large window offering a grandstand view of the excavations. A push-button control allows us to start a tape-recorded commentary. After a moment it is easy to identify how the remaining walls map out the living quarters to the right, with dormitory and refectory, and stretching away on the left the long nave of the priory church, with the choir, presbytery and lady chapel beyond it. The commentary recounts for us the cycle of worship of the canons of the order, from Prime at sunrise to Compline at sunset, with one-and-a-half hours of Matins and Lauds between midnight and about half-past-one in the morning.

The museum is set in extensive wooded gardens in a sweeping landscape, with a herb garden and fish pond. Amongst the attractions to be discovered by visitors exploring a little are a walk along a stream through a glade of azaleas, and two small summer houses. One is 18th century, a model of simplicity, the other Victorian, with 'Hansel and Gretel' gothic windows. You can also see a replica of a 13th century monastery bell. The pit in which bells were cast was uncovered during the excavations, revealing enough fragments of one of the moulds into which the molten metal was poured to enable a new mould to be made. Platts of Widnes cast a bell, Manchester Ship Canal hung it up, and Sir Bernard Lovell rang it for the first time, in 1977. Now you can too.

ST HELENS

Pilkington Glass Museum

Prescot Road, St. Helens, Merseyside WA10 3TT
(0744) 692499 curatorial enquiries;
(0744) 692014 general enquiries
Closed mornings on Saturdays, Sundays and Bank Holidays.

🚻 🅿 ♿

🚹 & 🚻 groups of more than 12 should book in advance, in which case catering may at certain times be provided by arrangement, in Pilkingtons' staff restaurant; phone for details, and for information about educational materials and film showings. Evening opening for groups by appointment.

The first Pilkington to concern himself with glass, over a century ago, was a doctor, who found that selling the wines and cordials he recommended was a better line than medicine, and then that making the glassware to sell them in was a better bet still. The firm have often shown the same imagination since, as when they established their museum, opened in 1964, and got the innovative museum designer, James Gardiner, to design it for them. Nobody has done more than Gardiner in introducing lively contexts and understandable information in museum displays. Pilkington's display includes models, several life-size, to convey the techniques of glasswork of every age, besides collections presenting the art and science of the business. Some of Gardiner's ideas are beginning to be adapted in turn now, but the displays at Pilkingtons have been kept up-to-date, both from the point of view of display and of the glass technology on show. The museum also keeps adding to what is already one of the finest collections of historic glassware in the country.

Glass is basically molten sand, or silica, and may even be made naturally

Aquatic Life, *etched cameo glass bowl by George Woodall at Thomas Webb & Sons, 19th century*

when lightning strikes a beach. Manufacture of glass by man depended on mixing silica with something that lowered its melting point before the sustained high temperatures to melt silica in quantity were possible. Soda, derived from burning plants or wood, was most commonly used by early craftsmen. The secret of glassmaking was discovered early, and wonderful glassware was made in the ancient Near East and Rome. Examples from many parts of the ancient world are on show here. Perhaps the loveliest glassware still looks like liquid. The ancient glassmakers rarely failed to retain this quality, as they drew out long necks of glass for flasks, which would resist the evaporation of their contents, or twisted and folded mixtures of coloured glass into marbled shapes, for bottles of rare, exotic scents. The Romans, given to dull pomp in so much of their art, presided over a whole empire of glassmaking that has never been surpassed.

It was only rivalled by the Venetians in the 16th century, with a glassware so light that it can be like tableware made of films of liquid, like soap bubbles, supported on columns of transparent threads. A hexagonal-topped glass in this collection is one example. Soda glass, however, could be affected by moisture. It was George Ravenscroft in late 17th century London who finally discovered the trick of making a heavy, solid glass, which was robust yet brilliantly transparent, by adding lead to his mixture. Many 18th century English drinking glasses, with tubes of air or coloured glass trapped in their stems, and twisted into nesting spirals, made the most of the properties of this new material.

There are all kinds of techniques for ornamenting glass. Additives to the mixture give rich, glowing colours. The Bohemians became masters of coloured glass, imitating the Venetians. Glasses of different colours can be made to flow together. The Venetians established a virtuoso tradition in this line, which survives there still on the island of Murano. One technique involves making thin rods of glass with twisting coloured inclusions, then reheating rows of them placed side by side to make sheets of complex spiralling patterns, for blowing into the form of goblets or plates. In the cameo technique, a decorative design can be revealed when parts of a surface layer of glass are ground down, or etched away with acid, to reveal as background a lower layer of another colour. Other examples of engraving displayed include an English 18th century glass with its stem cut into curved diamond facets, and its bowl decorated with a picture made up of tiny stippled dots by a Netherlandish specialist. A modern masterwork of craftsmanship for enthusiasts of clear cut-glass is a large, minutely-cut vessel on which the finest blowers and cutters of Waterford glass collaborated in 1987.

Late 16th century 'latticinio' goblet made in Southern Europe, possibly Murano

'Dromedary' flask, Syria, 6th–8th century AD

Glass for windows, ordinary and not-so-ordinary, has always posed technical challenges. A bow window in the displays downstairs, looking out onto a scene, illustrates the story of steadily increasing clarity and flatness, pane by pane. Early window panes depended on the skill of blowers, who could spin an open bubble of glass into a flat disc. Small, relatively flat and clear rectangles could be cut from this disc, which was known as crown glass. The lumpy bullion of glass left at the centre of the disc was sold off cheaper, and is still to be seen in many old windows. Larger sheets were made by blowing long cylindrical tubes, which could be cut along their length and flattened. The glass for the Hall of Mirrors at Versailles in the 17th century, and the Crystal Palace in the 19th was made like this. By the beginning of this century, the industry could handle colossal tubes, forty feet long. Heavier sheets of plate glass were poured on flat surfaces, or squeezed out between rollers, until in the 1950s Pilkington's began to float a continuous ribbon of glass on the surface of huge pools of molten tin. It took years of courageous persistence to make the transition from the demonstration of feasibility to profitable production.

Looking through the periscope

Downstairs, too, there are some entertaining applications of glass. The famous Victorian conjuror's demonstration, Pepper's Ghost, is explained here, and there is a distorting mirror. One firm in east London still makes these, solemnly catalogued as 'Number so and so, very small head, very long body, very small feet'. Other displays are more technological, coming up-to-date with holograms and fibre optics. You can even look through a twelve-foot periscope at what's going on in Pilkington's headquarters all around you, a crystal clear view through two prisms and thirteen lenses, most of them made of more than one piece of glass. Find out what it feels like to swivel it around like the submarine captain in so many films. Those handles either side of the eyepiece do not just swivel it, the left hand one angles the view skywards or downwards, and the right hand one changes magnification. When you have finished, you can snap the handles up against the body like those captains do, but you cannot slide this tube up and down. It would also be a mistake to scream 'dive, dive, dive' as you do so, because this periscope was actually made for the bridge of a 1950s frigate, to survey operations on deck from the open bridge during bad weather or battle.

SALFORD

Salford Art Gallery and Museum

Peel Park, Salford,
Greater Manchester M5 4WU
(061) 736 2649/737 7692
Closed Saturdays. 🇫 ▣ 🅿 ♿
♿ & ♿ book in advance by phone.

Two specialities distinguish Salford's Art Gallery and Museum. One is a row of Victorian shops and domestic interiors, displayed as brightly lit scenes, glimpsed through windows looking onto a darkened street reconstruction, along which visitors may stroll. This kind of display was pioneered in England at York Castle, but Salford's version is a successful adaptation of the idea. The grittier record of the local scene in more recent times, which occupied L.S. Lowry for a lifetime, provides the other special attraction; nowhere else has such a large collec-

tion of his work usually on show. Salford also has some good Victorian pictures, and a varied programme of art exhibitions, mostly of contemporary or earlier 20th century work.

The Victorian pictures have recently been redisplayed, and many have been cleaned and restored. 'Famine' by J.C. Dollman is the most striking. The figure of Death strides across a snowy landscape at the head of an army of wolves, crows flapping along as a vanguard. It is not the kind of thing most folk would want for their lounge, but the blanched tonality and somewhat subdued atmosphere are an appropriate hors d'oeuvre for Lowry. First of all, however, there was a bit of light relief on the landing when I visited, in the form of a display of mechanical musical devices, from musical boxes to pianolas. In the earlier boxes the tune was played by a stubble of bristly spikes on the surface of a cylinder, each spike carefully placed to twang just the right prong of a metal comb at just the right moment, as the cylinder revolved. The 'Sublime Harmonie' box of 1893 had a repertoire including Rossini, Strauss

L. S. Lowry, The Lake, *1937*

Interior of the Corner Shop, Lark Hill Place

and Gounod, whilst the 'National' offered such airs as 'Gladys', 'Flowers of Edinburgh' and 'The Bogeyman'. Later versions replaced the cylinder with paper tapes, or a choice of changeable disks, so that the repertoire was less limited. If you want to know what they sounded like, put 10p in a slot in the Polyphonium downstairs in the Victorian street.

Many of the Victorian painters employed much skill in making the physical qualities of their paint as unobtrusive as possible, to concentrate attention on the illusory effects of light and distance in their pictures. In the work of L.S. Lowry, every brushstroke is obvious. There are no show-off effects. The pictures are held together overall by his curious invention of keeping the ground and the sky all of one tone, often of the same colour, grey in the earlier works, increasingly white thereafter. The pictures are deceptive in many ways. They look drab, but there is often much colour painted into them at a detailed level. The brushstrokes appear dead-pan, without Van Gogh-style swirls, but any painter in oils will sympathise with Lowry's delight in getting the thickness and texture of the paint just right for the strength of local tone or colour. Lowry's pictures lose a great deal in reproduction, because of the loss of this paint texture. Most deceptively of all, his style looks like caricature, but it gives a view of the urban landscape of the Lancashire cotton industry that seems more and more expressive as a true portrait as the years pass by.

The people in Lowry's pictures were more important to him than the industrial landscape in which they appear. He is famous for painting 'match-stick' figures, yet he was a master of body language. In his drawing 'On the Sands' of 1921, compare the personalities of the three men walking to the left in the foreground. At first sight they seem to be marching along as inexpressively as soldiers on parade, but little differences betray whole personalities. A number of the figures in this early drawing are gesturing to one another – one boy and girl are even arm in arm. In Lowry's later work, the body language is less and less that of people communicating one to one, unless you count the man ramming a bowler hat over his opponent's head in 'The Fight'. In the crowded townscapes, people are either lost in the crowd, like the streaming figures, all leaning forward, in 'Coming from the Mill' of 1930, or else they are isolated by some gross idiosyncrasy, often, in the later paintings, a physical disablement. His representations remain sympathetic, though. There is even a self-portrait in the same vein, with the artist shown as a lazy figure, lying on a wall with his bowler on his stomach whilst the world works in the background. Lowry loved people, and although he was undoubtedly an emotionally imprisoned man, who detested anything demonstrative or theatrical, he was warm and far from friendless. The warmth comes across in his recorded statements about life and art, on show with his pictures in this display.

Lowry might not have liked the theatricality of 'Lark Hill Place', the Victorian street reconstruction downstairs, but many of the fittings in the shops have been rescued from real premises. It is evening, and the lamps are lit. Sounds fill the air – horses' hooves, chimes, a barrel organ, hammering and bells. We can peer into two parked carriages. The interior of the

closed one is tiny, yet four passengers might have travelled in here. People were smaller then, on average, but even so, you would have had to make a special booking if you wanted to take your knees along with you. The windows of the many business premises are full of clues to a vanished way of life. In the Cobbler's, a notice announces a rise in prices, with effect from 6th February 1892, for the knockers-up who banged on your windows in the morning, tuppence a week for a knock between four and seven in the morning, fourpence for three to four o'clock, 'yours truly the knockers-up of the district'. There are more discoveries to be made in the toyshop, tobacconist's, milliner's, chemist's, grocer's, the pub and others. You can also put 10p in a slot to operate a pier-end entertainment. A house catches fire and glows, gates open, and a fire engine crawls out, whilst, incredibly slowly, a fireman inches up a ladder.

Advertisers in those days did not dilute the message. 'What is the most useful thing in the world?', asks a sign in the grocer's, 'Hudson's Extract of Soap'. The message was not always so bland. In the Chemist's window we can study the seven overwhelming reasons for keeping Fenning's Stomachic Mixture handy. It was good for faintings, low spirits and 'nervous feelings', but the really important thing was the Cholera. Looseness of the bowels was the first sign, usually striking at night, and, without Fenning's to the rescue, that was likely to be it. 'The penalty of not having the medicine in the house ready to take at a critical moment might be DEATH.' This was a good marketing theme, apparently, or at least it also appealed to the makers of the energising food supplement, Virol. 'Mothers, look to this,' says their card, 'of 541,487 people who died in England in 1897, 231,607 were children. Poverty of the food given is the main cause. Virol may save your child's life. Try it!' A touch of that kind of thing would bring a bit of much-needed Lowry-esque grit to those happy-family breakfast cereal advertisements on television. Real fibre, or else.

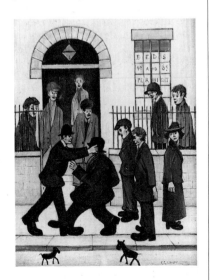

L. S. Lowry, The Fight, *c.1935*

Salford Museum of Mining

Buile Hill Park, Eccles Old Road, Salford M6 8GL
(061) 736 1832
Closed lunchtimes. 🅵 🅿
♿ S: part of ground floor accessible to wheelchair users. ♿ & ♿ phone to book, and for information about services.

Salford's Museum of Mining has been installed successfully in recent years in a villa in a municipal park. It is full of real objects rescued from the industry, but displayed in a way that is quietly dramatic, as well as informative. The cellars of the house have been taken over for scaled-down reconstructions of coal mines of different periods, and the first floor presents a lively, modern display of the history of coal and mining from Roman times. The museum also houses an extensive photographic and documentary archive, of which part is usually on display.

The reconstructed mines are in two sections. The first, at the entrance to the museum, is a short length of tunnel, with glimpses to left and right of a cramped stall at the coal face, and an inclined 'mainriding' tunnel. This display is separated from the main section by a reconstruction of pit-head offices for a small mine. The effect is suitably dismal, with small-scale colliery equipment all around. You can peer into the entrance, to the rudimentary washing facilities. The manager's office is also fairly sparse, with a canary in a cage, a plan of the mine, and copies of *Practical Coal-mining*, in an attractively embossed turn-of-the-century style cover. Round the corner in the lamp station, constant reminders about the need for safety only serve to emphasise the ferocious accident rate of the industry in former times. The miner's oil lamp was the vital indicator of a build-up of gas. A big poster of 1969 shows you just how the flame should look in different conditions. One safety reminder is quaint. A little glazed case on the wall displays a stick of explosive, looking

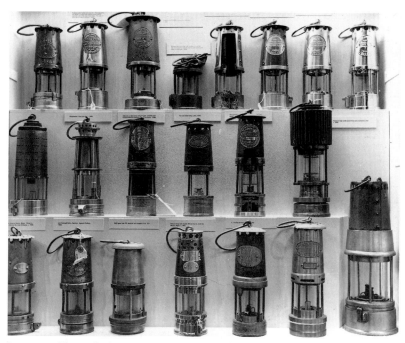

Later types of flame safety lamp

Drift mine entrance reconstruction

appropriately like a stubby firework, with a note beside it in a large, copper-plate hand: 'If you ever find anything like this,' it says, 'take it at once to your foreman and handle it with care.' Safety posters of the 1970s pulled no punches. A realistic picture of a mangled figure trapped in a coalcutter disc acted as a reminder to 'Look, see, listen, and only then switch on'.

Stairs descend to the main reconstructions. These have been built with expert help, and are too realistic to be completely free from hazard (a notice advises anyone a bit unsteady to give them a miss). On your way down, you can pause to unhook the earpiece of a robust wall-mounted 'phone, and turn the handle to make a call. Further on is the first of three commentary boxes, activated by pressing a button. A voice explains the view alongside, into a 'stall' of 1850 or so at the coal-face. A boy of perhaps no more than ten would have drilled into the coal seam a hole for a small explosive charge, whilst the collier cut out a cavity of coal at the foot of the seam. When the charge was detonated, the rest of the coal collapsed into the gap, for gathering into the tubs – small trucks on rails – and dragging out. All being well. The people involved were instead quite often blown up or buried in the process.

The next commentary point explains the coalface of the 1950s. Telescoping hydraulic steel supports and steel beams have replaced the wooden ones of the earlier stall, and the cavity at the bottom of the face is now cut by a type of giant chain saw. A coal seam can be imagined as a huge slab, perhaps 200 yards wide, extending for miles, and just thirty inches to five foot or so high, lying between other strata like a slab of cheese in a sandwich. The coal face is one end of the slab. By the 1950s, the cutter hauled itself on a steel cable along all 200 yards of the face, cutting a cavity at the base. Then the coal above was blasted down, just as in the earlier stall. In this reconstruction, the cutter, with its winching gear and a conveyor belt to carry out the fallen coal, is to our right. As the process trimmed off the end of the face, like someone taking a thin slice off the slab of cheese, the miners advanced the long line of support posts, one by one. As they advanced them, the part of the roof that had been supported simply caved in. We see the result to our left, a long low waste, as it is known, filled with a sloping pile of rubble. This would have been a relatively luxurious face: you can almost stand upright in it. More commonly, you would have had to crawl through the space between the supports, sometimes wriggling through when the rubble to the left spilled into the gap.

After the coalface, a third commentary point explains the blasting of roadways to and from the face through solid rock. Explosive packed into concentric rings of holes was detonated at half-second intervals to fragment twelve-foot diameter circles of rock with successive zones of compression and release. We emerge, past a view into a firemens' (colliery officials) room, with more warning posters, and, back on the ground floor, a reconstruction of a pit-pony dragging a tub out of the sloping entrance to a drift mine.

Selections from the photograph archive are displayed in a gallery that also serves as a film theatre, and up the staircase. Photographs in mines posed special problems. The risk of explosion made lighting a test of ingenuity, and it tended to be difficult to back away from the subject enough to include much in the view. A master of the art was Frank Grimshaw, to whom a display was devoted at the time of my visit. His camera was displayed – an Envoy

Pit wheel and cage from Wood Pit, Haydock, in Lancashire

STYAL

Quarry Bank Mill

Styal, Cheshire SK9 4LA
(0625) 527468
Mill open daily June to September, closed on Mondays October to May. Apprentice House not always open; limited number of timed ticket holders admitted at any one time. 🚻 ▣ 🅿
♿ S: but special route for disabled visitors; leaflet on access and facilities available on request.
🏨 & 🍴 must book, in which case they may be admitted from 9.30am; phone for details, especially for Apprentice House; no groups admitted on Sundays.

At the heart of the 250 acres of attractive National Trust country park at Styal is the complex of mill buildings that Samuel Greg began to build in 1784. They are extensive, yet almost tucked away, in a ravine cut by the drop in the river Bollin which attracted Greg to the site: it meant that water-driven power for the mill could be readily harnessed. Now the buildings house one of the most convincing industrial heritage sites in the country, still under development but already offering a wide range of spectacular displays, with working machines, enthusiastic demonstrators in period costume, and excellent visitor facilities.

An audio guide to a model upstairs from the entrance provides an overview of the site and its history, before we cross a high walkway above the main courtyard into the introduction. Panels here relate the triumphal foundation and colossal growth of the cotton industry. Not everyone welcomed it. The established woollen interest had it put about that 'the wearing of cotton promotes erotic feelings in chaste women'. Perhaps that was the secret. By 1860, it is estimated that the industry supported some 20% of the population of England, supplying, thanks to a bit of imperial arm-twisting, the majority of

from the '50s, with a special lens to give an angle of view of over ninety degrees. Grimshaw's photographs showed Old Meadows Colliery in 1969. Some of the coal had still to be hacked out by hand, and other pictures record the backbreaking work of pushing the 'tubs' of coal along low passages, and taking coal out by hand. Grimshaw also followed the miners home, all the way to the bathtub by the hearth. There were, in addition, even earlier photographs displayed, taken by J.C. Burrows with a large-format plate camera in the last century. Burrows used a powder flash system, in mines with no risk of explosion. Other photographers recorded groups of miners, and of the famous pit-brow lasses, the women who did heavy work on the surface. A more recent photograph showed one of England's smallest mining operations just before closure in

1981, Ludworth Moor Colliery, with owner and sole miner Geoff du Feu taking out coal by hand in a two-foot high seam.

The first-floor display tells the story of mining, from its beginnings with the formation of the coal itself. There are samples of coal of different types, including the Peacock variety, infused with a rainbow irridescence. Coal can be remarkably beautiful underground. The displays include large relics: a horse-gin, used to winch miners up and down in early workings; a small iron cage from a later shaft; and the cutter disc from a modern coalcutter, with ferocious teeth set in a brilliant red spiral of steel. There are dozens of other curious objects as well, used to bring to life a documentary display that is interesting just to wander through, and extremely informative if you have a little time to spare.

the world's need for cotton cloth.

Upstairs we discover the cottage industry, which developments like Greg's supplanted. Here are the basics: raw cotton, spinning wheels and their accessories, and cottage looms. You will find a spinner here too, and a weaver, working the machines and able to supplement the information on the panels. You can watch how since antiquity cotton was drawn out by spindles falling under their own weight, until the spinning wheel was introduced, reaching England in about the fourteenth century. The cotton had first to be combed, or 'carded' to line up the fibres, before the long tubes of soft cotton could be spun. It was a complex process, and it took eight spinners to produce the thread for one weaver, even a weaver using hand-looms like the ones you will see working here. If

you have never quite got the hang of how a loom works, offering alternate tunnels of warp threads for the torpedo-like shuttle to zoom through to and fro, leaving its trail of thread, this is your chance to find out.

After displays highlighting water-power technology, we discover downstairs the first of several rooms full of the giant, frenetic machines that progressively mechanised those basic cottage processes on a larger and larger scale. Here is the Self Acting Mule, Slubbing Frame, Carding Engine, and looms like the Northrop, of the 1890s. Thanks to a sculptural arrangement of nested umbrella shapes at one end, the latter could even feed the whizzing shuttle with freshly charged 'pirns', the spindles from which the weft thread spools out continuously from inside the shuttle, whenever that thread ran out.

Demonstration of hand spinning

There is a reminder of the operatives who worked in this room, in the form of a privy; it worked on the medieval, oubliette principle.

We pass through rooms explaining the finishing processes – bleaching, printing and dyeing. There is a photograph of William Perkin, intense and aesthetic-looking at the age of eighteen, when, as modelled in a life-size reconstruction here, he stumbled across the separation of aniline from coal-tar and founded a huge industry of synthetic dye manufacture. Perkin's purple, it seems, was just what the market had been waiting for. Other reconstructions explain textile printing processes.

We descend to a contrast. First, documentation, mementoes and reconstructions conjure up the privileged, if caring, in a patrician way, lives of the Greg family. Greg's wife Hannah compensated for some of her husband's sternness, questioning his conviction that novels and literature could have no place in the life of a man of business, and insisting on attention to the spiritual welfare of the workforce. We can follow the family's fortunes through four generations, and

Children recreating lives of apprentices in the Apprentice House

then pass on to the contrasting life of the operatives. Greg's workers, in rural conditions, were a lot better off than their colleagues in the execrable, utter misery of towns like Manchester, but it was a hard life of twelve-hour days from the age of eight. The peak of skill for anyone who did not become a foreman commanded little over a pound a week in 1830, usually much less.

Just how hard the life could be we get an inkling of when we proceed into the weaving shed. We are advised to linger here no longer than fifteen minutes because of the noise of the looms, yet only a handful are working compared to the dozens of a century ago. Their action is frenzied, leather

Exterior view of Quarry Bank Mill, Styal

Demonstration of weaving

thongs whipping the shuttles to and fro through the warp like loony automata playing ping-pong. There is just space between the forest of rollers and levers for the operative to walk, but he or she needs to be wary. Especially in the last two hours of a twelve-hour shift, workers exhausted by noise and labour suffered dreadful injuries, some chronicled here. Even bigger machines live in the room below, the long mules, which did the work of hundreds of spinners, with some 120 feet of machinery, roll-

ing backwards and forwards on delicate spiral-spoked wheels.

All the machinery depended on the power supply, and we descend finally to a huge water wheel, twenty-two feet wide, twenty-four feet in diameter, magestically turned by the waters of the Bollin, as they drop thirty feet from a murky pool in the cellars. Teeth on the giant wheel engaged gears, which transmitted power up shafts through the whole building, though not so reliably as to avoid the need to install steam engines as well, before being replaced by turbines.

A five minute walk from the mill brings us, with another ticket, to the whitewashed house that Greg built in 1792 for his apprentices. Fire and structural safety requirements limit visits here to thirty people at a time, so a visit must be booked, for a particular time. Yet eighty children, from eight to

eighteen, lived and slept here. They were from orphanages and workhouses, and were a commodity so sought after by mill owners they had to be found as far away as London. Greg's were relatively well off, with even a little education thanks to Hannah, but they worked a twelve-hour day, on a diet of little more than thin porridge and potato pies. Here, costumed interpreters reconstruct for us their daily lives, in schoolroom and kitchen, with one pump in the yard for any bathing or washing for all eighty of them, and straw beds in the dormitories, each for a pair of children. Did they find comfort in those beds, or tryanny in whatever society grew up amongst the eighty children there, overseen by one man and his wife? It is fascinating to have even a glimpse of the intense young lives that must have been lived out in this house.

WARRINGTON

Warrington Museum and Art Gallery

*Bold Street, Warrington, Cheshire
WA1 1JG   (0925) 30550/(0925) 35961*

Closed Sundays. **F**

& **S**: wheelchair access to first-floor level by service lift, by prior arrangement; balcony displays inaccessible.

& phone Education Officer to book, and for information about extensive services and activities.

Warrington Museum manages to be an unusually lively and imaginative place whilst remaining that rare treasure, a museum of museum practice. The borough was one of the first in the country to set up a museum on the rates, and opened its purpose-built galleries in 1857. It took advantage of the collections of the Warrington Natural History Society, and the scientific collections remain a great strength, although now supplemented by curious social and local history collections, excellent ceramics and glass, and some paintings and sculpture. A number of displays are being modernised, and the museum has a good record for buying in, or devising on only a modest budget, exhibitions with unusually popular appeal.

The great rarity to be found here, however, are educational scientific displays of an antiquity second to none. In these departments Warrington held out against the reckless insistance on being new-fangled, which swept away generations of such displays in other museums during the last seven decades. Only an occasional gesture to modernisation was admitted, leaving a hint of what might be the 1930s here, or the '50s there. Through parts of this museum, curators seem to have passed whole careers leaving only the mercifully light touches of ghosts.

The geology room on the first floor is the most splendid example. Cases

'Who Killed Cock Robin' (representing the trial of the Hon Grantly Berkeley for cockfighting)

William Reynolds-Stephens, Guinevere's Redeeming, *1905*

around the walls relate the geology of the area, whilst desk cases in the room centre present mineralogy. The room is two stories high, with a balcony at the upper level that has an elaborately decorative cast-metal railing. Beneath it, over the geology cases, dinosaurs lumber around in monochrome pictures on a set of panels angled downwards for easy viewing. In the geology cases there are many fossils. Most are indecipherable to a non-specialist eye, but it is worth looking out for delicate, recognisable shapes. Best of all is an amazing tangled mass, several inches across, of what look like tassels, until you notice that every tassel is scaled like a lizard's toe. This is a Crinoid, *Pentacrinus fossilicis Blum*, and the long cords that snake out of the tangle to isolated tassels are the remaining tentacles. Crinoids, undersea creatures, generally had five tentacles, and trapped food with the tassels on their ends.

Mineralogical specimens, like the ones in the room centre here, can look daunting to a lay eye, except for a few pretty ones; but if you are not a specialist, look out for two rarities. One is a fan made of dozens of tiny blades of carved slate, each thin as a leaf, with delicate edging and fretted holes. Slate carving like this was done by workers in the North Wales slate quarries. This

View of the Geology room

however did she come by such a thing?) There are many beautiful things in here, too, amongst artefacts from pre-historic Europe, and from later cultures all over the world. The Peruvian pottery, in this room and next door, is especially good. The next room contains local bygones of all kinds, and beyond it are the rooms used for the lively programme of temporary exhibitions, and the ceramics gallery.

The balconies of these rooms display botany, fish and reptiles. Like the lower scientific displays, they are backed up by a venerable litter of the most ancient labels and pages from books. There are also enchanting models in all these rooms. The ones for geology are of wood and varnished composition, whilst archaeology benefits from a miniature cut-away demonstration of a bronze-age burial, which looks just like a sponge-cake with tiny skeletons baked into it. In Botany there is a set of models to demonstrate the sex-lives of plants on scientific principles in the Prussian manner, by R. Brendel of Berlin, antiques in their own right.

Half way up the stairs between these galleries and the balcony level is a room of much more up-to-date zoology, with details of the distinguished naturalists who have worked in the area. There are good displays of birds and eggs, and amongst the exotic specimens are a pair of magnificent male birds of paradise, displaying their courting feathers. One imaginative window shows a slob's larder, spilt food and upset garbage everywhere, being enjoyed by every variety of pest, a sort of nightmare international conference of them, including moths, bed-bugs and cat fleas, but concentrating on beetly things. There is an Australian Spider Beetle, of course, Museum Beetles, obviously, and a whole army, presumably demented, of Confused Flour Beetles. Opposite is an eccentric tableau, using stuffed creatures, of the celebrated rural trial of the Hon. Grantley Berkeley, for participating in cock-fighting, before magistrates whom the whole district knew to be his regular companions in the sport. The accused, water-rat, is pinioned by lowering game-cocks before the owl

specimen, more a whole helix than a mere fan, is a masterpiece of the craft. The other item is a small, shiny, irregularly edged metallic disc. This is a section through a meteorite found in Devil's Canyon, Arizona, in 1891, which has been polished, then etched lightly, so that in its gleaming surface you can see the regular crystal patterning of the iron within.

One exit from this room currently leads to more recent displays of human physiology and natural history, including a charming Pangolin, a creature whose scales are shaped to make it look like a walking artichoke with a long nose. These are shortly to be changed for social history displays. Beyond is a small art gallery. If instead of going on to it you return from geology to the staircase, you will find across the landing another high, balconied gallery, containing human artefacts and remains from all over the world. There are graveyards with fewer human remains in them than can be seen in this gallery: heads shrunken in Ecuador, the lips pierced with pegs; or decorated by the Maoris of New Zealand, skulls festooned with feathers and string. It takes a moment to remember that these are the remains of people, and that it could be a bit of you there in the showcase.

This is easier to imagine in the case of the complete Egyptian mummy, which has been scientifically chronicled so that we know he was a boy of about fourteen. (It was 'given by Mrs. Higginbotham' – very nice of her – but

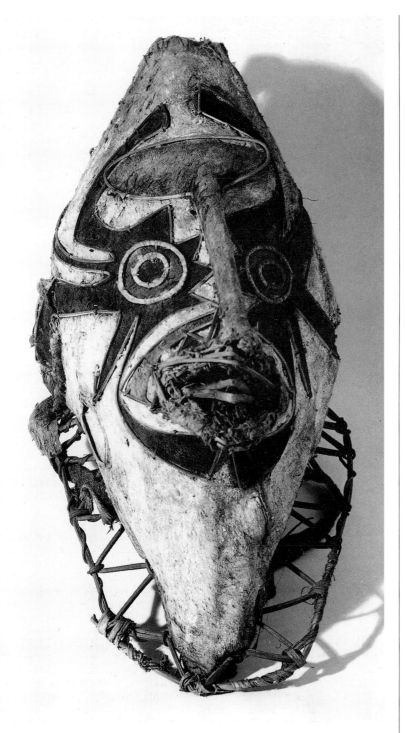

New Guinea Spirit Mask

judges, with farmer hedgehog and bad characters magpie, hawk and jay looking on, amongst many others.

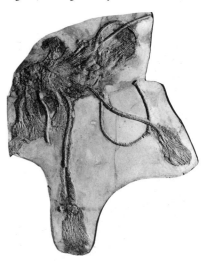

Crinoid Pentacrinus fossilicus Blum

The glass and ceramics are at the back of the museum. Glass was a speciality industry in Warrington, and the collection is being redisplayed on the balcony level. The ceramics are in regularly refurbished displays at the back of the main floor, and are strong in English earthenwares, including Wedgwood. There is a fine array of teapots from 1700–1820, besides teasets, jugs and mugs. A popular curiosity nearby is a colour lithograph, dating from the middle of the last century, showing three pictures, which present themselves one by one as you move around it: first some flowers, then a portrait, then a dog appear, by a clever arrangement of strips against a printed background. On your way in and out of the museum, there are Victorian oil paintings on the staircase, including local scenes, and some sculpture. On the main-floor landing is King Arthur's 'Guinevere', by the Art Nouveau-period sculptor, William Reynolds Stephens. It shows the taste of the period for unrestrained mixtures of precious-looking materials, silver and copper as well as bronze, with ivory for face, hands and tiny toes, and mother-of-pearl decorative inlays.

WIDNES

CATALYST:
The Museum of the Chemical Industry

Gossage Building, Mersey Road,
Widnes, Cheshire WA8 0DF
(051) 420 1121
Closed on Mondays, except Bank Holidays. 🏧 ⬛ due to open 1992.
🅿️ ♿W
🚻 & 🚻 must book in advance.
Scheduled to open mid-June 1989.

CATALYST: The Museum of the Chemical Industry, is not just the first museum devoted to its subject. It is also probably the first museum in the world to try putting visitors in a glass case, to look at historical material left outside. The case, an elegant high-tech steel and glass viewing platform, was built by an unusually imaginative council a couple of years ago, on top of a building that once served as the nerve centre of the largest soapworks in the world. The area onto which it looks out, spread out along the Mersey below and reaching to the horizon on every side, is the historical heart of England's chemical industry. The visitors will not be alone in their glass box, however: collections of historic material relating to the industry are being added to innovative interpretative displays, due to open in mid-June 1989 as just the first stage in ambitious plans for development of the whole building, and the surrounding site.

Chemical engineering is perhaps the least known form of heavy industry, yet all the others depend on it. Most of us have a stereotype view of pallid boffins at the lab. bench, peering out through webs of weird piping connecting bubbling globular retorts. That is about spot-on, but here in Widnes we can see the business scaled up to production level. Near the museum entrance are some of the huge vessels in which the reactions on this scale were staged. Large wooden vats sufficed for the low-energy processes of the 19th cen-

Aerial view of the CATALYST site

tury. But an eight-foot-deep bulging pot of steel, several inches thick, shows the kind of thing needed to contain the reactions our consumer world depends on. Its interior is massively ribbed, to help stir up the reagents.

A lift, which rises a hundred feet in a square tube of glass, brings visitors to the observation platform. The view is dominated by the Mersey, spreading to

Detail of steel reaction vessel

A chemical works laboratory

east and west in gleaming ribbons across broad sweeps of estuary sand, pinched by the prominence of land on which Widnes reaches out to its neighbour across the water, Runcorn. This is the geography that attracted the early industrialists, well formed for transport of the few staples of industry in those days – coal, salt and limestone – and for distributing the products made, chiefly alkalis and acids.

It is an industrial landscape with a character of its own, which has had no Lowry to paint its portrait. Chimneys and churches protrude into the skyline, as they would in a panorama of cotton mills, but in a broad sweep from north to west the scene assumes a character peculiar to the chemical industry, a three-dimensional snakes and ladders of openwork scaffolds, supporting cat-walks and metal-runged stairs around pipes, vessels and retorts as big as buildings. ICI, BOC and Laporte's are amongst the continuing operations here, making all those substances we seem to need, chemicals for non-stick saucepans, Paraquat for the garden, and vinyl chloride for PVC, as well as older staples, caustic soda and sul-phuric acid.

To the east, smoke and steam pour from the chimneys and giant cooling towers of the largest power station in the North West, whose name, Fid-dler's Ferry, recalls a smaller and now forgotten enterprise on this site by the banks of the Mersey. The scene is threaded with relics of the commercial war between different forms of 19th century transport, which followed prosperity here. A long, gently curving railway viaduct marches around from west to south on an army of narrow arches, to the turrets of what was, when built in 1869, the longest span of rail-way bridge in the world. The rail link it opened, between Widnes and Run-corn, is now completed by road with a magnificent green bridge of 1961, of just the arcing form as the one over Sydney Harbour. Opposite, to the north east, a spur from the St. Helens Canal comes to an abrupt end in the lock that connects it with the Mersey. Now pleasure boats crowd the canal, between green meadows where the de-relict buildings of the soapworks have been swept away around the new museum and the land reclaimed for recreation. Telescopes linked to taped commentaries help survey the view.

A photograph of 1920 shows the

area around the museum from the air when the soapworks, Gossages, were still a leading producer. Ranks of fac-tory buildings filled the triangular site, with this present one standing proudly at the apex. Now all that remains is a colourful assortment of samples of long-disappeared brands, such as Gos-

Precision chemical balance

sages Magical Soap, which will be displayed in a recreated 1920s shop in the museum's first gallery. This will show how the chemical industry in the area that is visible from the museum has changed over the last 150 years. The displays will be strong on innova-tive techniques, including computers to answer your questions about indus-try today, and to give you a chance to see what happens when you are left in charge of a production run. Videos will complement the photographs of the labs., plants and people who make up this industry.

In 1991 the second phase of the museum will open in the form of a 'Chemicals and Everyday Life' gallery. Computers, videos, recreated scenes and a range of working demonstrations will focus on the role played by the chemical industry in people's everyday lives, past, present and future. There will be a series of sections covering themes such as 'Keeping Clean', 'Staying Healthy', 'Food and Shelter', and 'Getting Around'. The 'Chemicals and Civilisation' experience opens in 1992, when visitors will be taken on a journey through time to explore the impact of the industry through a series of recreated scenes.

Bar and packet of Gossages' Soap

WIGAN

Wigan Pier

Wigan Pier, Lancashire WN3 4EU
(0942) 323666
(24-hour recorded information
0942 44888)
Open daily. 🚻 📷 🅿
♿ (special information leaflet
available from the Piermaster's
Office).
🚹 & 🚺 must book in advance to
get discount: contact Group
Bookings Officer for details of
charges and extensive facilities.

Wigan Pier was the end of the line for
coal trucks. It jutted just a few feet over
the canal, curving upwards and carrying two rails; trucks pivotted on it as
they tipped their load of coal into
barges. Tradition traces the name
'Wigan Pier' back to a railwayman's
joking response to a party of holiday-
making miners in a train stopped at
Wigan, who asked if they had arrived at
seaside Southport. The 'pier' was demolished, but a reconstruction has
been put back now, so that visitors can
wander down the canal and see it in the
course of a tour to the 'all singing all
dancing' heritage centre that has been
built around it. Almost literally 'all
singing and dancing', because your
visit is likely to be enlivened by the
company of actors who re-enact everyday life of turn-of-the-century Wigan
in the displayed reconstructions, as
visitors wander through. This part of
the visit, called 'The Way We Were', is
in a large warehouse at one end of the
site, and includes sections on holi-
daymaking, the world of work (with a
reconstructed coalmine), and domestic
life. The reconstructions gain authen-
ticity from the incorporation of a great
deal of original material, and all are
amply documented. A short walk
around the canals, or a ride on a
waterbus, brings you to Trencherfield
Mill, a huge cotton-spinning mill with
working machinery, where, if you ar-
rive at the right time most days, you
can watch engineers set in motion the

Canal boat, Wigan Pier

truly colossal steam engine that once
powered the whole building.

A visit to 'The Way We Were' begins at the seaside. On the left is the
business end of travelling there in the
form of a whole signal-box. Climb up
into it to see a plan of your section of
the line, with a vintage signalling device to keep you and everyone else
clear about whether there is a train on
the line or not, and forty big levers to
make sure they all do it your way.
Downstairs there is a passengers'-eye-
view as well, from an old compartment,
before you get down to the serious
business of seaside entertainment. It is
all here, from Punch and Judy to a
fortune teller, who reveals her crystal
ball in response to a coin in the slot,
with a number of 'What the Butler
Saw' machines to peer into. Turn the
handles for views of elaborately-clad
bathing beauties.

Round the corner, the world of work
is waiting. 25,000 Wigan men worked
down the pits by 1900, and as you
thread your way down the narrow passages of the reconstructed coal mine,
glimpses on either side hint at harsh
working lives. Dimly lit contorted

Punch and Judy

bodies were squeezed into spaces that
were sometimes little more than cran-
nies, in the struggle to get enough coal
into each tub to support a family. Only
the coal in that tub counted for wages;
getting ready, walking to the coal-face,
even underground, setting up the sup-

ports for the roof, finding bits of rail to get your tub to where you were working, waiting for the fireman with the explosives – none of it was paid. The miner even had to hire the vital lamp that warned of deadly gas. The lamps and identity discs provided cover for a sometimes fatalistic attitude to safety, tellingly revealed here in employers' statements after the Maypole Pit disaster. No wonder that when baths were first provided in 1912 many were too hardened to see the point. One is quoted here: 'I thowt as on'y as were 'enpecked at home was usin't baths.' Many women worked in the industry, too, and are commemorated in the reconstructions. They were the pit-brow lasses who hauled coal on the surface, and became famous because they held a titillating attraction for a number of Victorian men.

Many other trades, including the workings of the warehouse, are evoked by reconstructions, photographs and displays. Elsewhere, real rescued fittings provide the background to life at home, in the pub, and at school. The latter is where the acting company stage what is currently their most popular routine, so if you want to experience the firm hand of a bit of Victorian discipline be sure to book your desk. With numerous daily performances, there is usually room if you book early. If you do not get in, you will still find plenty going on in the other settings; and if you want a bit of peace, you will find a quiet chap to share it with, in the outside privy. Amongst the real-life experiences to be discovered in the documentation are reminiscences in letters home from the Boer War, like this one, from a picture-framer's son: 'It makes a fellow feel funny when the bullets are flying over his head . . . one cannot see the shot, but the whistling of them makes a fellow almost cringe. Of course, that is only at first.' Even the picture-framers were tough in Wigan.

Trencherfield Mill, across the canal at the other end of the site, was a spinning mill. The cotton came here in the form of imported bales. As it passed from machine to machine, cotton fibres – cloudly, fragile ropes of them –

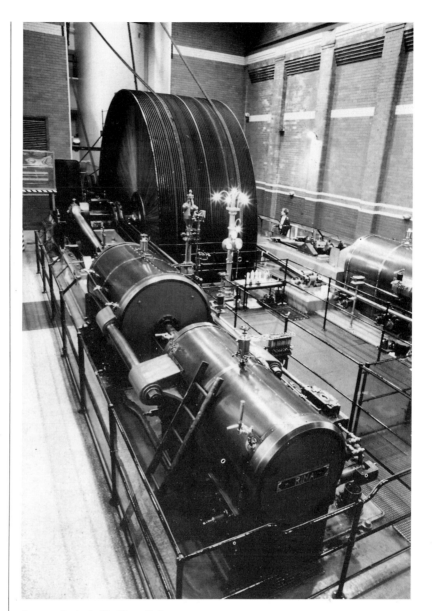

Steam engine in the Machinery Hall

were teased from the bale, then successively twisted and stretched into ever finer and stronger thread. A mill like this spun miles of thread every few seconds, on machines like the ones that engineers keep working here, components moving faster than the eye can see. There are also two steam engines in the main hall, one of which drove a

giant fan, which ventilated a nearby colliery, and now sits outside the Mill like a piece of sculpture. The flywheel of each engine was cast in just two great sections, and there is no problem about seeing how the whole thing was put together, with giant nuts and bolts. There is also equipment from a rope-walk at nearby Leigh in this hall. It is

Actors playing a Temperance scene

still not at all easy to see how a bit of rope was put together, until you watch the video that reveals all.

For a grand finale, a flight of stairs leads into the hall, which houses the steam engine that supplied power to the whole mill. In a mill like this, whatever machine you were working was powered just by a belt, driven by a spindle running along overhead. The spindle was turned by a wheel at one end, driven in turn by a rope from the steam engine wheel. This steam engine, of 1908, is a real whopper, with a wheel twenty-four feet in diameter. It drove a multitude of thick ropes, which you can see snaking away up a shaft running the full height of the building, to drive the smaller pulley wheels for each floor. The engineers set it in motion by using some of the steam pressure to power a small engine, which engages cog-wheels around the big wheel. With the wheel slowly turning, one engineer spins what looks like a ship's wheel, to get the mighty pistons going. Deep sighs, gurgles and puffs of steam emerge from the gleaming brasswork; the wheel gathers speed, but it is only when your eye follows a point on one of the ropes that you realise the rate at which it is now turning.

WINDERMERE

Windermere Steamboat Museum

Rayrigg Road, Windermere, Cumbria LA23 1BN (09662) 5565
Closed from November to Easter.
🚻 🖼 🅿 ♿ W
🏛 & ♟ must book to be sure of an illustrated talk and guided tour; other special facilities can also be booked: phone for details. ☺

Within ten years of opening, Windermere Steamboat Museum now houses boats from the 18th century to thoroughbred speed machines, many of them in immaculate working order. The displays illustrate the rich and colourful history of Lake Windermere and of the vessels in the collection, within a large building adjacent to which is a wet-dock full of boats. The steam-boat trips on the lake depart from the jetty by the boathouse.

The history of Windermere, and of its well known characters, is intriguing. The steam-boats were not welcomed, especially by the gentry, when the 'Lady of the Lake' initiated the first commercial service in 1845. The opposition to the boats was lampooned in *Punch* with a poem: 'What incubus, my Goodness, have we here / Lumbring in the bosom of our lovely lake? / A steam-boat as I live! – Without mistake! / Puffing and splashing over Windermere! / What inharmonious shouts assail mine ear / Shocking your echo that perforce replies, / "Ease her!" and "Stop her!", – frightful horrid cries / mingling with frequent pop of ginger beer ...' The great poet Wordsworth declined his invitation to the opening, although earlier he had written a poem, also quoted here, not unsympathetic to the machines. It is curious that now the machines that Wordsworth called 'harsh-featured' appear old world and charming.

The earliest boats in the museum comfortably pre-date steam. There are the remains of a yacht of 1745, clinker built, with overlapping planks, and a near-perfect hull of a yacht of 1780, carvel built with flush planks. Clever use of large sail-shaped panels on the walls give an idea of the size of both. There are mementoes of the new steamers, which came to replace the old ferries, or were used as luxury boats by the wealthy. Colonel Ranelagh's steamyacht, 'Brittanic' was bigger than some Atlantic steamers, and

Interior view of the boathouse

Miss Windermere IV

A relic from the 'Britannic'

relics of her lavish furnishings are here. A Falcon 2 glider hangs from the ceiling, the first to be launched successfully from water. There is a group of craft built for racing or speed trials, the Chris Craft speedboat, 'Jane' of 1938, Norman Buckley's 'Miss Windermere IV' of 1958, and the hydrophone racing boat, 'Cookie', of 1962. Biggest of all, on loan when I visited, was the BBC's replica of the 'Bluebird', originally of 1952, which flipped over at 320 mph or so in 1967, killing Donald Campbell. It was a real bit of 1950s technology, a tiny pilot's cockpit with one huge dial showing speed, plus some stabilisers painted blue, strapped onto a jet engine. The film of Campbell's speed-haunted life in which this replica appears, starring Anthony Hopkins, was broadcast in 1988.

The personalities of Windermere are endearing. You can try to outstare a photograph of PC Greenbank, Windermere's first policeman, who, they say, could control every situation with those burning eyes. Beatrix Potter, like her character Jeremy Fisher the frog, loved to go fishing, and here is her

rowing boat. Perhaps the most astonishing character was the inventor, J.G.A. Kitchen, a humorous, kindly, profoundly ingenious man, who secured 175 provisional patent applications – conferring the seal of originality as well as commercial protection – between 1891 and 1936. Kitchen was nothing if not original. He experimented for years on aeroplanes enclosed by completely circular wings, one of them a bi-plane visible in a photograph here. He delighted in being wheeled over his rockery in a prototype of his elliptical-wheeled wheelbarrow. His designs for elliptical-wheeled bicycles, barrows, tanks and trains did fall back ultimately on boring old round wheels, but only to drive a flexible steel, rubber-coated elliptical wheel running around them. As early as 1904, Kitchen and a friend, Isaac Storey, contrived to steer a boat around the lake by radio remote control.

The museum actually possesses one of the 'Flame-ophones' made to Kitchen's design, in which the vibrations of the needle playing a gramophone record changed the sound of flames in

thin rod gas burners. In the version on show, sound made by the burners was amplified by a metal reflector, but later versions had horns. The idea did not catch on, although the horned versions anticipated a fundamental element of recent speaker design: there were separate horns for the bass and treble components of the sound. One invention did take off, the reversible rudder. It made some money, but one suspects that Kitchen really valued it for allowing him to play the game of sailing at full-speed towards an obstacle, then

The old ferry with a coach aboard

S. L. Kittiwake

The Isle of Man
DOUGLAS

The Manx Museum

Crellin's Hill, Douglas, Isle of Man
(0624) 75522
Closed Sundays. **F**
AT: wheelchair access to much of building (including lecture theatre); assistance provided, as far as practicable, with stairs elsewhere.
& must book in advance with The Secretary.

As this guide goes to press, the Manx Museum is in the middle of a complete transformation. A new extension is nearing completion, beside the small hospital building that has housed the museum since 1922. The extension, due to open in August 1989, will provide space for the island's art collections and education facilities for the museum, and will also offer special 'high-tech' attractions for visitors. The lecture theatre is being fitted with a giant screen laser-disk-driven video

Scale model of the Gokstad Viking ship, one of the types of ship used by visiting Vikings

stopping his boat dead in its tracks by reversing the rudder, or of turning his boat around in its own length.

We pass through a passage to the shop, and on to the large, airy wet docks. Each boat has its own personality. S.L. 'Branksome', in teak with walnut panelling, velvet upholstery, carpets and marble wash-basin, is the most luxurious steamboat of her kind surviving anywhere. 'Lady Hamilton' has a hand-cranked gramophone aboard, with a stack of 78 rpm records. Beatrix Potter got a bit upset by people playing wirelesses and gramophones on the Lake. M.V. 'Canfly' is a speed-boat, her Rolls-Royce Hawk engine originally made in 1917 for an airship. Her six gleaming cylinders, adding up to 7.4 litres, are open to the air, and give Canfly a top speed of 30 mph. 'Dolly', according to the Guinness Book of Records, is the oldest mechanically-powered boat in the world. 'Esperance', with 'bows like the bows of an old-time clipper and a stern like that of a steamship', according to the children's novelist Arthur Ransome, was the houseboat of the character Captain Flint in his classic children's Lake District boating yarn of the 1930s, *Swallows and Amazons*.

system, to be used initially for a twenty minute dramatised presentation of the history of the island. Another video installation will invite visitors to select, by referring to a large scale relief model of the island, sequences of film on topics of interest. The opening of these displays is just one stage in the updating of the museum over the next few years, which will transform the present displays to provide a detailed chronological look at the island's history, from prehistoric times to the Manx TT races, with the natural environment as a centrepiece.

The first gallery, showing the island's prehistoric past, was opened in 1986. It begins with 'a slice through time', an imaginary section through an excavation site, showing the scale and sequence in which evidence of the past typically lies concealed. The 10,000 years since the last Ice Age are packed into eight feet of soil layers, distorted by uplifting of the ground and by human activity. Embedded in the earth, around and beneath the points of posts holding up a strand of barbed wire at the top of the section, we see the litter of many generations, from stone implements to modern vessels, with hints of more dramatic remains, a great prehistoric deer, and Viking and Christian burials. Nearby, the whole skeleton of a real prehistoric stag, perhaps 8,000 years old, with magnificent antlers that seem to flow rather than to have grown, presides over this display.

Through to the left are shown 10,000 years of the real thing, past a case that describes the practicalities of archaeology. In the course of the display, the techniques are explained that gave to stone tools, earthenware vessels and early metalwork the forms that we see in the specimens here. The successive adoption of these materials summarises generations of early human settlement. They mark off stages, from the lifestyle of the early hunter-gatherers, through the first agricultural settlements to the evolution of a socially stratified society. If you arrived in Douglas by air, you will already have visited the site of one early, simple farm dwelling, whose contents are displayed in the museum; it was disco-

Thistle-head brooch from the Douglas Treasure Hoard

Skeleton of the Great Deer

Calf of Man Crucifixion carving, probably an altar frontal, first half of 9th century AD

navia, certainly did not. Coin hoards and spectacular burials characterise their contribution. Every hoard would tell a story if it could, probably of a sad, failed attempt to preserve the modest wealth of a whole lifetime of effort through some terrifying episode of disruption, like the troubled reign of Sitric Silkbeard, who tried to hold sway in these parts when one hoard was buried. The Douglas tresure hoard is the richest, including magnificent large brooch cloak-fasteners of silver (although not all the finds in the hoard ended up in the museum). Other articles from the Viking period commonly survived because they were buried in the graves of important figures in society, for their use in the afterlife.

A burial is reconstructed for us in the displays, just as archaeologists uncovered it. Here lay a warrior, the hilt of his rusted sword still showing its gleaming inlay of the finest silver strapping. Such swords were treasured possessions, but the ones in these burials were broken into three pieces, perhaps to deter grave robbers. Animals were sacrificed over this warrior's grave, it seems, and, as was sometimes the Vik-

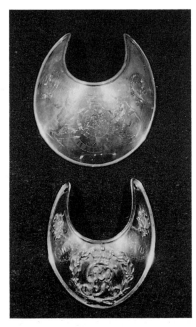

Gorgets associated with the volunteer Manx fencibles, Napoleonic War period

vered during construction of the runway at the airport. The display ends with the grave-marker stones that characterise the Celtic traditions that came to dominate island society in early modern times, and finally with early Christian remains. One of these is a great treasure, a delicate stone low relief carving of the early ninth century, used as the centrepiece of an altar front, and showing a stylised view of the crucifixion.

The displays of later island life on the main floor of the museum are to be transformed, but existing installations show some of the material available. The Romans passed the island by, but the Vikings, sailing down from Scandi-

Reconstruction of the kitchen of a Manx farmhouse

lanterns and one tiny window in the several-feet-thick wall. Hooks for the lanterns and for herbs hang from the raftered roof, the floor is stone flagged, and the furniture is of great simplicity.

The museum also has extensive natural history collections, with a grand whale skeleton, many seabirds, and a seal. The art collection is comprised of work by Manx painters and pictures of local scenes and people. There are two unusually complete late-18th century sets of the latter, by the minor watercolourists Moses Griffiths and John Warwick Smith, commissioned at a time when the geography and antiquities of the island began to appeal to the romantic imagination. The John Warwick Smith set in particular shows the island as it still appears today – beautiful green rolling hills, with only occasional settlements, spectacularly rocky coasts and ancient sites.

A gallery has been installed recently for small temporary exhibitions on various themes.

The Manx Museum includes a library, and performs for the Isle of Man the functions overseen in the United Kingdom (of which the Isle of Man is not a part) by National Heritage, the National Trust and other environmental heritage authorities. In addition, it runs several other museums on the Island (see list at the back of this volume).

ing custom, a young woman as well. The back of her skull was completely removed by the blow that killed her. Traces of another sacrificial female were found at Chapel Hill, Balladoole, but a third woman, known as the 'Pagan Lady of St Patrick's Isle (or Peel Castle), fared better. She was among many intriguing finds in a cemetary excavated recently at Peel Castle, a stronghold on the far side of the Island from Douglas. The unknown woman, thought to be a Celt (as she lacked typical Viking ornament like brooches) was buried with her cooking spit, cloth shears, comb and a fine necklace of coloured glass and amber beads, with no two out of over sixty beads the same (at least on my brief inspection).

The museum has much evidence of life in the calmer times that slowly became the norm. Notable are the simple requirements of metal mining on the island; a miner's lamp on display is merely a candle stuck into a lump of clay on the front of a home-treated felt hat. An oddity is the sundial that John Kewley created for the Speaker of the House of Keys and installed in the latter's garden in 1774. It bristles with vanes, told the time in several parts of the world, and has verses in Latin, English and Manx inscribed upon it.

The Manx ones say, 'Cur Geil da'n Sca / Shen myr ta'n Tra', which sounds much more fun than the English 'Whilst Phoebus on me shines, / Then view my shades and lines'. It is currently shown in the museum basement, with other collections concerning fishing, farming and domestic life, and reconstructed interiors, which are expected to remain here after the reorganisation of the displays. The showpiece is the Manx Farmhouse, an interior of great charm, lit by candles,

Carved oak chest of 1641 owned by the family of the museum's first director, P. M. C. Kermode

OTHER MUSEUMS IN NORTH WEST ENGLAND

ASHTON-UNDER-LYNE

The Museum of the Manchesters
Ashton Town Hall, Market Place,
Ashton-under Lyne, Lancashire
(061) 344 3078
correspondence to: Libraries and Arts
Department, Tameside Borough
Council, Stamford House, Jowett's
Walk, Ashton-under-Lyne,
Lancashire OL7 0BB
(061) 343 1414

Presents the social as well as military history of a regiment.

BACUP

Bacup Natural History Society and Folk Museum
24 Yorkshire Street, Bacup,
Lancashire OL13 9AE
(0706) 876488

Collections of natural history and bygones of this local history society.

BARROWFORD

Pendle Heritage Centre
Park Hill, Barrowford, Nelson,
Lancashire BB9 6JQ
(0282) 695366

Four historic buildings, with displays on the history of the family and estate associated with them, and on life in the area.

BARROW-IN-FURNESS

The Furness Museum
Ramsden Square, Barrow-in-
Furness, Cumbria LA14 1LL
(0229) 20650

The history of Barrow-in-Furness, with special emphasis on ship-building.

BLACKBURN

Lewis Museum of Textile Machinery
Exchange Street, Blackburn,
Lancashire
correspondence to: Museum and Art
Gallery, Museum Street, Blackburn,
Lancashire BB1 7AJ
(0254) 667130

Collections of looms and other textile machinery, with a gallery for temporary exhibitions.

Sunnyhurst Wood Visitor Centre
Sunnyhurst Wood, Darwen,
Blackburn   (0254) 71545
correspondence to: Museum and Art
Gallery, Museum Street, Blackburn,
Lancashire BB1 7AJ
(0254) 667130

Displays about the history and natural history of the area.

Witton Country Park Visitor Centre
Preston Old Road, Blackburn,
Lancashire BB2 2TP
(0254) 55423

Displays of horse-drawn vehicles and of implements, with a natural history room and changing temporary exhibitions, in renovated stable buildings.

BLACKPOOL

Grundy Art Gallery
Queen Square, Blackpool, Lancashire
FY1 1PX   (0253) 23977

English painting, mostly 20th century, and some applied art.

BOLTON

Bolton Steam Museum
The Engine House, Atlas No. 3 Mill,
Chorley Old Road, Bolton BL1 4LB
correspondence to: Mr. E. Harris,
Curator, 57 Sheriff Street, Rochdale,
Greater Manchester OL12 6QR
(0706) 58528

A collection of the 'stationary' steam engines (that is engines for powering mills rather than steam locomotives) rescued from Lancashire mills by the Northern Mill Engine Society.

Hall i'th' Wood Museum
Green Way, Off Crompton Way,
Bolton BL1 8UA   (0204) 51159
correspondence to: Museum and Art
Gallery, Le Mans Crescent, Bolton,
Lancashire BL1 1SE (0204) 22311

Displays about local history, especially relating to Samuel Crompton, who lived in this timbered Tudor and Jacobean house. Some 18th century interior furnishings.

Local History Museum
Little Bolton Town Hall, Saint
George's Street, Bolton BL1 2EN
correspondence to: Museum and Art
Gallery, Le Mans Crescent, Bolton,
Lancashire BL1 1SE
(0204) 22311

Local history and industry displays in an old Town Hall and court building.

Smithills Hall Trailside Museum
Smithills Dean Road, Bolton
BL1 7NP   (0204) 41265
correspondence to: Museum and Art
Gallery, Le Mans Crescent, Bolton,
Lancashire BL1 1SE
(0204) 22311

Oak furnishings in a 14th–16th century house, with a fine Great Hall.

Tonge Moor Textile Museum
Tonge Moor Road, Bolton BL2 2LE
(0204) 21394
correspondence to: Museum and Art
Gallery, Le Mans Crescent, Bolton,
Lancashire BL1 1SE
(0204) 22311

Important historic early textile machinery.

Turton Tower
Chapeltown Road, Bromley Cross, Nr
Bolton, Lancashire BL7 0HG
(0204) 852203

correspondence to: *Lancashire County Museum Service, Stanley Street, Preston PR1 4YP*
(0772) 264061

A part timber-frame house originally of *c.* 1420, which has been home to several major figures in Lancashire's history and is now furnished with characteristic Lancashire items.

BURNLEY

Museum of Local Crafts and Industries

Towneley Hall, Burnley, Lancashire BB11 3RQ
(0282) 24213

Displays about the industries of Victorian and Edwardian Burnley, especially cotton and mining.

Queen Street Mill

Harle Syke, Burnley, Lancashire BB10 2HX   (0282) 59996

Traditional Lancashire cotton weaving in a preserved installation of looms, along with displays about the industry and the people who worked in it.

Weavers' Triangle Visitor Centre

85 Manchester Road, Burnley, Lancashire BB11 1JZ
(0282) 53007

Weavers' triangle is an area of canalside buildings, and displays in the old canal toll building explain the area and the cotton industry.

BURY

Bury Art Gallery and Museum

Moss Street, Bury, Lancashire
(061) 705 5879
correspondence to: *Libraries and Arts Department, Textile Hall, Manchester Road, Bury BL9 0DR*

Good collection of Victorian oil paintings and watercolours, including works by J.M.W. Turner. Local history, with reconstructions presenting everyday life in Bury.

The Museum is likely to be closed for building repairs and display renovations until at least early 1990. Phone to check.

Bury Transport Museum

Castlecroft Road, off Bolton Street, Bury, Lancashire BL9 0LN
(061) 764 7790

Historic road vehicles, along with railway locomotives, rolling stock and equipment.

Museum of the Lancashire Fusiliers

Wellington Barracks, Bury, Lancashire BL8 2PL
(061) 764 2208

History of the Regiment.

CARK-IN-CARTMEL

Craft and Countryside Museum

Holker Hall,
Cark-in-Cartmel,
Nr Grange-over-Sands, Cumbria LA11 7PL
(044853) 328

History of craft specialities in the area, including fishing, horn and slate working.

Lakeland Motor Museum

Holker Hall,
Cark-in-Cartmel,
Nr Grange-over-Sands, Cumbria LA11 7PL
(044853) 509

Vintage motors, with unusual collections of petrol pumps and memorabilia of the petroleum business, including a recreation of a garage of the 1920s.

CARLISLE

Guildhall Museum

Greenmarket,
Carlisle, Cumbria
correspondence to: *Museum and Art Gallery, Tullie House, Castle Street, Carlisle, Cumbria CA3 8TP*
(0228) 34781

Collections relating especially to medieval Carlisle, with civic memorabilia.

Museum of the Border Regiment and King's Own Royal Border Regiment

Queen Mary's Tower, The Castle, Carlisle, Cumbria CA3 8UR
(0228) 32774

History of the Regiments, with displays of booty from many parts of the world.

Prior's Tower Museum

The Cathedral, Carlisle, Cumbria CA3 8TZ
(0228) 25195/35169

Memorabilia of the history of the cathedral and the associated priory from Roman times to the 20th century.

CARNFORTH

Steamtown Railway Museum

Warton Road, Carnforth, Lancashire LA5 9HX
(0524) 732100

Collections of locomotives and rolling stock on a large site, including historic railway buildings.

CHESTER

Cheshire Military Museum

The Castle, Chester CH1 2DN
(0244) 327617

Collections displaying the history of the 5th Royal Inniskilling Dragoon Guards, the 3rd Carabiniers, the Cheshire Regiment and the Cheshire Yeomanry.

CHORLEY

Astley Hall Museum and Art Gallery

Astley Park, Chorley, Lancashire PR7 1NT
(02572) 62166

16th century furnished house with special collections of Leeds ceramics.

CLITHEROE

Clitheroe Castle Museum
Castle Hill, Clitheroe BB7 1BA
(0200) 24635
*correspondence to: Lancashire County
Museum Service, Stanley Street,
Preston PR1 4YP   (0772) 264061*

Geological, archaeological and later
collections presenting the history of
Clitheroe and the Ribble Valley.

CONISTON

Brantwood
Coniston, Cumbria LA21 8AD
(05394) 41396

Paintings and memorabilia of Ruskin
in a house that he lived in and rebuilt to
his own design.

The Ruskin Museum
The Institute, Yewdale Road,
Coniston, Cumbria
*correspondence to: Mr. J. Dawson,
Parkside, Haws Bank, Coniston,
Cumbria LA21 8AR   (05394) 41387*

An assembly of photos, documents and
memorabilia of John Ruskin, as well as
of Donald Cambell, and the history of
Coniston.

CREWE

Police Museum
Force Training Centre, Nantwich
Road, Crewe, Cheshire CW2 6NT
(0270) 500005

Small collection of policing equipment.
By appointment only.

ECCLES

Monk's Hall Museum
42 Wellington Road, Eccles, Greater
Manchester M30 0NP
*correspondence to: Salford Museum
and Art Gallery, Peel Park, The
Crescent, Salford M5 4WU*
(061) 736 2649

Collections of dolls, toys and games,
with some social and industrial history
items, in a part timber-framed house.
  Closed indefinitely from 1989;
phone to enquire.

FLEETWOOD

Fleetwood Museum
Dock Street, Fleetwood FY7 6AQ
(03917) 6621

Ship models and fishing equipment in
displays about the history of Fleetwood
and the fishing industry.

GISBURN

Tom Varley's Museum of Steam
Todber Caravan Park, Gisburn, Nr
Clitheroe, Lancashire BB7 4JJ
(02005) 322

Fairground steam engines and traction
engines.

HAWKSHEAD

*The Beatrix Potter Museum
and Hill-Top House*
Nr Sawrey, Hawkshead, Cumbria
(09666) 269

The Beatrix Potter Museum, installed
in her solicitor husband's premises in
Hawkshead, contains memorabilia and
displays a few-dozen out of a collection
of hundreds of her drawings. Her
house, Hill Top, a few miles up the
road, remains as she left it at her death.

JODRELL BANK

Jodrell Bank Visitor Centre
Jodrell Bank, Nr Macclesfield,
Cheshire SK11 9DL (0477) 71339

Jodrell's huge radio telescope dish and
smaller historic antennae preside over
documentary displays about
astronomy, especially radio astronomy,
but including a planetarium and
'hands-on' exhibits to explain the
science.

KESWICK

Keswick Museum and Art Gallery
Fitz Park, Keswick, Cumbria
CA12 4NF   (0596) 73263

Natural history, and especially geology,
with a huge (3-inches-to-the-mile)
model of the Lake District, besides
archaeology, and a special collection of
literary manuscripts of the romantic
poets.

The Pencil Museum
The Cumberland Pencil Company,
Greta Bridge, Keswick, Cumbria
CA12 5NG   (0596) 73626

Historic specimens, manufacturing
equipment and curiosities of this
industry, in the town that pioneered
the manufacture of graphite pencils in
the 16th century.

LANCASTER

The Cottage
15 Castle Hill, Lancaster
*correspondence to: Lancaster City
Museums, Market Square, Lancaster,
Lancashire LA1 1HT*
(0524) 64637

Furnishings of a working family home
of the early 19th century, with
documents about the history of the
building.

LEYLAND

*South Ribble Museum and Exhibition
Centre*
The Old Grammar School, Church
Road, Leyland, Lancashire
(0772) 422041

Roman archaeology and collections
illustrating local history.

LIVERPOOL

Croxteth Hall
Croxteth Hall Lane, Liverpool,
Merseyside L12 0HB
(051) 228 5311

Furnishings and fittings to show Edwardian life upstairs and downstairs, inside the house and in the outbuildings, based on a house of which parts date back to 1602.

Hornby Library

Liverpool City Libraries, William Brown Street, Liverpool L3 8EW
(051) 207 2147

Illustrated books.

Museum of the School of Dental Surgery

University of Liverpool, School of Dental Surgery, Pembroke Place, Liverpool L69 3BX
(051) 709 0141

Specialised collections for the profession (or brave members of the general public interested enough to make a *prior appointment*).

Sudley Art Gallery

Sudley Hall, Mossley Hill Road, Liverpool L18 8BX
(051) 724 3245

Some outstanding English pictures, including major paintings by Turner and Gainsborough, and 19th century pictures and furnishings.

Tate Gallery, Liverpool

Albert Dock, Liverpool, Merseyside L3 4BB   (051) 709 3223

Temporary exhibitions of national and international importance, along with selections from the permanent collections of the Tate Gallery in London, which houses the national collections of English painting, most of the Turner bequest, and Western contemporary art.

University of Liverpool Art Gallery

3 Abercrombie Square, Liverpool L69 3BX   (051) 794 2347

Liverpool University's collections of fine and applied art, which are strong in English porcelain and in 18th, 19th and 20th century English oil paintings and watercolours.

MACCLESFIELD

West Park Museum

Prestbury Road, Macclesfield
(0625) 24067
correspondence to: Macclesfield Museums Trust, Roe Street, Macclesfield, Cheshire SK11 6UT
(0625) 613210

Collections of local and natural history.

MANCHESTER

Fletcher Moss Museum and Art Gallery

The Old Parsonage, Wilmslow Road, Didsbury, Manchester M20 8AU
(061) 445 1109
correspondence to:
Manchester City Art Galleries, Mosley Street, Manchester M2 3JL
(061) 236 9422

Furnished house, with displays from the collections of the City Art Gallery.

Greater Manchester Police Museum

Newton Street, Manchester M1 1ES
(061) 855 3290

'Black' Museum of crime, plus police equipment.
By appointment only.

Heaton Hall

Heaton Park, Manchester M25 5SW
(061) 773 1231
correspondence to: Manchester City Art Galleries, Mosley Street, Manchester M2 3JL
(061) 236 9422

18th century house, with furniture and pictures of the period, and displays of other material from the collections of Manchester City Art Gallery.

Manchester University Medical School Collections

Stopford Building, Oxford Road, Manchester M15 6BR
(061) 275 5035

Specialist collections of historic medical equipment, mainly for the profession.
By appointment only.

Museum of Transport, Greater Manchester

Boyle Street, Cheetham Hill, Manchester M8 8UL
(061) 205 2122

Large collection of historic public road transport vehicles, along with memorabilia of the business of running them, in a real old public transport bus garage.

Wythenshawe Hall

Wythenshawe Park, Northenden, Manchester M23 0AB
(061) 998 2331
correspondence to:
Manchester City Art Galleries, Mosley Street, Manchester M2 3JL
(061) 236 9422

Restored Tudor mansion, with interior furnishings mostly in the Victorian Jacobean-revival style, and displays of material from the collections of Manchester City Art Gallery.

MARYPORT

Maritime Museum

1 Senhouse Street, Shipping Brow, Maryport, Cumbria CA15 6AB
(0900) 813738

Personalities and historic items from the history of a seafaring town.

MILLOM

Millom Folk Museum

St George's Road, Millom, Cumbria LA18 4DD
(0675) 2555

Artefacts and bygones of life and industry in the area, with reconstructions of an iron-ore drift mine and a miner's cottage.

NANTWICH

Nantwich Museum

Pillory Street, Nantwich, Cheshire
CW5 5BQ   (0270) 627104

Collections of local and social history, with the cheese industry as a speciality.

NORTHWICH

The Salt Museum

162 London Road, Northwich
CW9 8AB   (0606) 41331

Pictures, reconstructions and some historic artefacts presenting the history of the staple industry of the town, from pre-Roman times onwards.

Stretton Mill

Stretton, Farndon, Cheshire
(08298) 276
correspondence to: Cheshire Museums,
162 London Road, Northwich,
Cheshire CW9 8AB   (0606) 41331

Watermill, originally of the 16th century, with equipment in working order and displays about the business of milling.

OLDHAM

Saddleworth Museum and Art Gallery

High Street, Uppermill, Oldham
OL3 6HS   (04577) 4093

Collections of local history and lifestyles, along with geology and natural history, in old watermill buildings. Art Gallery for exhibitions of work by local artists.

PENRITH

Penrith Museum

Robinson's School, Middlegate,
Penrith, Cumbria CA11 7PT
(0768) 64671

The history of Penrith and the Eden Valley, with collections of archaeology, natural history, geology and bygones.

PORT SUNLIGHT

Port Sunlight Heritage Centre

PO Box 139,
Greendale Road, Port Sunlight,
Wirral, Merseyside
L62 4ZP
(051) 644 6466

The life and industrial career of Lord Lever, of 'Sunlight Soap' fame, with drawings and records of the development of his concept of Port Sunlight Village.

RAVENGLASS

Muncaster Mill

Ravenglass, Cumbria CA18 1ST
(06577) 232

Working 19th century water-driven corn mill.

Railway Museum

Ravenglass and Eskdale Railway
Company Ltd.,
Ravenglass, Cumbria
CA18 1SW
(06577) 226

History of the Ravenglass and Eskdale Railway (on which visitors may still ride) in an old railway station.

RIBCHESTER

Ribchester Museum of Childhood

Church Street, Ribchester, Lancashire
PR3 3YE
(025484) 520

Toys, especially dolls and dolls' houses, from the mid-19th century onwards.

Ribchester Independent Museum of Roman Antiquities

Riverside, Ribchester, Lancashire
PR3 3XS
(025484) 261

Finds from a Roman fort are the main component of displays presenting Roman military life.

ROCHDALE

Ellenroad Trust Limited

Ellenroad Engine House, Elizabethan
Way, Milnrow, Rochdale, Lancashire
OL16 4LG   (0706) 881952
curatorial enquiries: phone Philip
Mills, evenings   (0706) 43169

Historic steam engines, including rarities, along with other engineering equipment, in an engine house that survives from a cotton mill.

Intermittent Sunday openings from Easter 1989, leading to full opening scheduled for summer 1990.

Rochdale Art Gallery

The Esplanade, Rochdale, Lancashire
OL16 1AQ   (0706) 342154

Collections of mainly English 19th and 20th century painting, but almost all display space is usually devoted to temporary exhibitions of contemporary art, with emphasis on equal opportunities issues in the arts and in society.

Rochdale Museum

Sparrow Hill, Rochdale, Lancashire
OL16 1QT (0706) 47474 ext. 4924

Collections of local history.

Rochdale Pioneers Memorial Museum (Toad Lane Museum)

31 Toad Lane, Rochdale, Lancashire
OL12 0NU   (061) 832 4300

Displays built around a reconstruction of the room in this building in which the Rochdale Equitable Pioneers Society opened the first outlet of what became the international Co-Operative Movement.

ROSSENDALE

Rossendale Museum

Whitaker Park, Haslingden Road,
Rawtenstall, Rossendale, Lancashire
BB4 6RE   (0706) 217777

Local natural, social and industrial history in a magnate's mansion.

ST HELENS

St Helens Museum and Art Gallery
College Street, St. Helens, Merseyside
WA10 1TW
(0744) 24061 ext. 2959

Local industrial and social history, with archaeology and natural history, and a gallery for exhibitions of work by local artists.

SALFORD

Ordsall Hall Museum
Taylorson Street, Salford M5 3EX
(061) 872 0251

A historic house with a fine Great Hall of the 16th century, and displays of later social and local history and industries.

SOUTHPORT

Atkinson Art Gallery
Lord Street, Southport, Merseyside
PR8 1DH (0704) 33133 ext. 2111

19th and 20th century English pictures, with some earlier ceramics, silver and glass. Temporary exhibitions of local and contemporary art.

Botanic Gardens Museum
Churchtown, Southport, Merseyside
PR9 7NB   (0704) 27547

Local history and everyday life, with historic vehicles and a natural history section.

STALYBRIDGE

Astley Cheetham Art Gallery
Trinity Street, Stalybridge
SK15 2BN
(061) 338 2708/3831
correspondence to: Libraries and Arts Department, Tameside Borough Council, Stamford House, Jowett's Walk, Ashton-under-Lyne, Lancashire OL7 0BB
(061) 343 1414

Temporary exhibitions of art and craft, mostly contemporary. Occasional displays from a permanent collection consisting mainly of 19th century painting, but also including a small group of 14th–16th century pictures.

STOCKPORT

Bramall Hall
Bramall, Stockport, Cheshire
SK7 3NX
(061) 485 3708

An outstanding tudor timber-frame house, with some historic furnishings and a room of unique 16th century interior wall paintings.

Stockport Museum
Vernon Park, Turncroft Lane,
Stockport SK1 4AR
(061) 474 4460

Displays of local prehistory and later social and industrial history.
    Undergoing extensive transformation in 1988-90, to provide visitors' centre-style displays about the Goyt Valley.

Stockport War Memorial Art Gallery
Wellington Road South, Stockport,
Greater Manchester
SK3 8AB
(061) 474 4453

Permanent collection of English 19th and 20th century pictures, and of European furnishings of the 17th and 18th centuries. Display space usually devoted to temporary exhibitions, mainly of art and craft.

ULVERSTON

The Laurel and Hardy Museum
4a Upper Brook Street, Ulverston,
Cumbria LA12 7BQ
(0229) 52292

A privately-owned museum of Laurel and Hardy memorabilia in the town in which Stan Laurel was born in 1890, with an archive of films.

Stott Park Bobbin Mill
Finsthwaite,
Newby Bridge,
Via Ulverston,
Cumbria LA12 8AX
(0448) 31087

Working machinery in a Victorian water-powered mill originally set up to make wooden bobbins for the Lancashire cotton industry, later diversifying into bobbin-making of all kinds.

WARRINGTON

Museum of the South Lancashire Regiment and the Lancashire Regiment
RHQ1, Queen's Lancs Regiment,
Peninsular Barracks, Warrington
WA2 7BR
(0925) 33563

Regimental history.

WHITEHAVEN

Whitehaven Museum and Art Gallery
Civil Halls, Lowther Street,
Whitehaven,
Cumbria CA28 7SH
(0946) 67575 ext. 31

Temporary installation of collections of archaeology, local pottery, iron and coal mining, and maritime history. Small temporary exhibition space, often used for photography shows.

WORKINGTON

Helena Thompson Museum
Park End Road, Workington,
Cumbria CA14 4DE
(0900) 62598

Collections of social history material and applied arts in an 18th century residence, with temporary exhibitions in the attached stable block.

Isle of Man

CASTLETOWN

The Nautical Museum
Bridge Street, Castletown, Isle of Man
correspondence and group bookings to:
The Manx Museum, Crellin's Hill,
Douglas, Isle of Man
(0624) 75522

Displays of the ships, equipment and
seafaring people of the area. The
centrepiece is a late 18th century
armed ship, the yacht 'Peggy', in her
original boathouse.

CREGNEASH

Cregneash Folk Museum
Cregneash, Isle of Man
correspondence and group bookings to:
The Manx Museum, Crellin's Hill,
Douglas, Isle of Man
(0624) 75522

Crafts and lifestyles of this Manx
fishing community, with live
demonstrations, in a group of
preserved cottages.

PORT ERIN

Aquarium
Department of Marine Biology of
Liverpool University, Port Erin,
Isle of Man
(0624) 832027

Displays of marine life and research
into it, with an aquarium of live
specimens.

RAMSEY

The Grove Rural Life Museum
Andreas Road, Ramsey,
Isle of Man
correspondence and group bookings to:
The Manx Museum, Crellin's Hill,
Douglas, Isle of Man
(0624) 75522

Furnishings and equipment of life in a
well-to-do household; outbuilding
displays of the equipment of larger
Manx farms, including the house's
original horse-powered threshing mill.

ISLE OF MAN

Ramsey

Port Erin   **Douglas**
        Castletown
Cregneash

● **Museums described**

○ Museums listed only
  (excluding town names
  already among museums
  described)
  Both refer to towns
  in which museums
  are located, not to
  the museums themselves.

● **Carlisle**

Maryport
            Penrith
Workington
         Keswick
Whitehaven

● **Grasmere**

Hacokshead
         ● **Windermere**
Ravenglass   Coniston
         ● **Kendal**

Millom
       Ulverston   Cark-in-Cartmel
Barrow in Furness   Carnforth

● **Lancaster**

Fleetwood   Gisburn
            Clitheroe   Barrowford
Blackpool   Ribchester **Padiham**
         Preston   **Burnley**
                        Accrington
         Blackburn
Leyland **Helmshore**   Bacup
                        Rossendale
Southport   Chorley   Rochdale
            Bolton Bury
Wigan   ● **Oldham**
                Eccles   **Ashton-**
St. Helens   **under-Lyne**
Liverpool   **Salford**   Stockport
Birkenhead **Prescot** **Manchester** Stalybridge
Port Sunlight **Widnes** **Warrington**
                Runcorn   **Styal**
Ellesmere Port
         Northwich   **Macclesfield**
● **Chester**   Jodrell Bank
         Crewe
         Nantwich

Manchester

Index of Subjects

Index of Museum Names

Printed in the United Kingdom for Her
Majesty's Stationery Office.

Dd.240078 8/89 C70